FULLY
BOOKED

The Formula For a Thriving Healthcare Business

BRETT CAMERON

WHY NOT HAVE BRETT CAMERON AS A GUEST SPEAKER ON YOUR PODCAST, SEMINAR, FESTIVAL OR INDUSTRY EVENT?

CAMERON HYPNOTICS – BUSINESS COACH AND MENTOR TO HEALTHCARE PRACTITIONERS

Tel: +61 403 335 751
Email: brett@cameronhypnotics.com.au
Website: www.cameronhypnotics.com.au

In 2006, Brett Cameron took a leap of faith to answer an inner calling. He left a successful and lucrative corporate career in sales and marketing, to pursue a dream to be his own boss in an industry that helps others.

Brett retrained as a Clinical Hypnotherapist and Neuro Linguistic Programming Practitioner. 14 years later, he is now a sought after Professional Practitioner operating a thriving Fully Booked Practice in Newcastle, Australia. He is a Mentor to Practitioners in the industry, a Keynote Speaker and Author.

BOOKS BY BRETT CAMERON

FULLY BOOKED
The Formula for a Thriving Healthcare Business

ONLINE PROGRAM BY BRETT CAMERON

Healthcare Business Masterclass

FULLY BOOKED

The Formula For a Thriving Healthcare Business

BRETT CAMERON

The Potentialist
by *Maggie White*

Mind Potential Publishing

Author: Brett Cameron
Title: Fully Booked
ISBN: Paperback: 978-1-922380-21-0
ISBN Kindle: 978-1-922380-23-4
Category: Business | Self-Help Techniques

A catalogue record for this book is available from the National Library of Australia

Publisher: Mind Potential Publishing
Division of Mind Design Centre Pty Ltd, PO Box 6094,
Maroochydore BC, Queensland, Australia, 4558.
International Phone: +61 405 138 567
Australia Phone: 1300 664 544
Publisher Website: www.thepotentialist.com

Cover design by NGirl Design | www.ngirldesign.com.au

DEDICATION

This book is dedicated to the inspirational women in my life.

I dedicate this book to both my dearly departed mum Audrey, and late wife Cynthia who, through her journey of healing, inspired me to become a hypnotherapist; and to my loving and supportive wife Afaf Girgis AM.

I have been blessed.

Contents

Foreword

You owe it to your clients to become massively successful in your healthcare business.

Consider the person who has been struggling with a problem. Maybe they've been living with a fear. Perhaps there's a habit that's been damaging their health. They are possibly stressed with a lack of confidence.

If your business is not yet living up to its full potential (and please note the word "yet"), this person may have to live with their challenge longer than necessary. Or worse, it may never be resolved.

Imagine the changes you'll create in the world as you've built a thriving "fully booked" business. Customers will easily locate you. They'll know you're skilled at the work you do. They'll feel confident and safe to pay an appropriate premium for your services. They'll get the help they need and enhance the quality of their life. They'll become a raving fan of the service you provide. They'll share their story with others. The changes they've created will inspire an exponential benefit to the world. More people will release what has been holding them back.

Your work has value. I suggest you take on the idea that's it's your moral obligation to better serve the world with your skills. You also deserve to enjoy a comfortable life of financial freedom along the way.

Fully Booked shares with you a step-by-step process to make growing a thriving healthcare business much easier. As Brett Cameron says, "it all begins with a dream." His inspiring story will show you why it became a burning desire to step away from a corporate career to build his own business as a Clinical Hypnotherapist. It's a natural transition that he expands this work from helping his clients to now help you create your own success.

What's your story? We all have our own origin stories as to why we first wanted to begin a career helping others. Please take a few moments to connect with the reasons why your journey began, and why you've picked up this book. You will easily stay inspired to put in the hours and the work necessary to grow your business as you keep your own story top of mind.

Brett guides you in the book, through a journey showing you what works to grow your business, while artfully shifting your thinking into a mindset for success. You will learn how to build a solid foundation for your business. You will discover proven methods to create a structure for a sustainable and secure future.

Brett is a model of someone who has done the work. He's put in the tens of thousands of hours discovering what works and helping thousands of clients along the way. He's been there. He's done that. Just like anyone in business, he's also made a few mistakes, He passionately and humorously shares these stories, so you don't have to make them yourself! This book will shorten your learning curve in building your business.

If your business is just getting started, you will benefit from learning the strategies that have been already proven to be successful. You will feel more confident taking your leap of faith into becoming an entrepreneur. There's no need to reinvent the wheel, and it's always best to model what's working right now in our industry.

Some of you already have successful healthcare businesses. The fact that you're reading this book means you realize there are possibilities to either grow further success or reach new audiences. Brett will help shift your thinking to discover new ways to streamline your success.

I first met Brett Cameron at a conference in Las Vegas. He had flown from Australia to the United States to network and learn from peers in our industry. I was teaching a workshop for hypnotherapists on how to attract clients who were willing to pay a respectful premium for our services. Brett was sitting in the front row taking notes on some of the business systems I shared.

I was in Brisbane in Australia a month later. This time, I was sitting in the audience taking notes when Brett was on the platform speaking on the monthly rituals necessary to grow a healthcare business. He immediately established himself as someone who had a mastery of his skills, a passion for helping others, and a desire to keep learning.

These stories prove that we all continue to learn. Your success will naturally continue to grow as you develop an ongoing passion for enhancing your knowledge. We all continue to grow as we learn from each other. The more we're all successful, the more we're all successful.

Brett is an expert in the field. The mark of a true professional is their willingness to share with others. He has proven this dedication by mentoring other practitioners and taking on a leadership role with the Australian Hypnotherapists Association. Remember that moral obligation to help others? As we step into a leadership role, the lives we enhance exponentially grow as there are more of us serving the world.

It's a perfect fit to learn business from such a successful hypnotherapist. We help facilitate mindset shifts with our clients by putting the right words in the right order at the right time. All communication is influential, so if you're going to be influencing, it might as well be done effectively.

You owe it to your clients to develop rock-solid business strategies so you can give them 100% of your focus and best help them.

You owe it to your clients to break past your old beliefs about money to respectfully charge a fair fee for your services.

You owe it to your clients to stand out from the crowd and sell the value of what you do.

You owe it to your clients.

Jason Linett
Director of Virginia Hypnosis (USA) and
www.worksmarthypnosis.com

Introduction

I have been in practice as a hypnotherapist and NLP practitioner since 2006. While I can now state with confidence that I have a successful business, it hasn't always been that way. I have had moments where the business was struggling, and as a result I was struggling. I have had moments wondering where the next clients will come from. Yet, I persevered and succeeded. I want to share some of those business lessons with you to help you build your successful business.

Over the recent years I have spoken with many healthcare practitioners who love the work that they do with a passion, yet their businesses are struggling. I've also spoken with students who have a dream of becoming a practitioner in their chosen field, however they have no idea how to start in business.

- These practitioners are competent, yet they struggle to attract clients/patients to their practice.
- They want to be fully booked, to have a reliable formula for a successful business.
- They have many unanswered questions as to how to get the business formula right.
- They are often overwhelmed when they think about how to market themselves and their business.
- They simply want a business that helps people and supports their personal needs too.

This book will give you solutions and also provide easy to follow interactive resources that will help you with business growth. It is a 'how to' guide to help healthcare practitioners and students to:

- gauge the fundamentals of business when setting up your practice in a way that is sustainable.

- develop a stronger branding presence.

- understand the changing world of marketing, sales and advertising

- understand their therapeutic small business in terms of tailored admin structure.

- have a deeper understanding of what you either bring or don't bring to the business.

- grasp the importance of and make the space for personal development and self-care (your business won't grow if you don't grow).

- remove the overwhelm. We've all been there, that feeling of, "I have no idea where to start so I'll just do nothing."

"The secret to getting ahead, is getting started." ~ Mark Twain

Fully Booked **is for healthcare practitioners who are:**

1. In an established business but growth has stagnated.

2. In an established business that's doing well, but who wish to move to the next level and want to know more about self-promotion and marketing.

3. Contemplating going into business as a healthcare practitioner, e.g. hypnotherapy, massage therapy, Reiki/kinesiology, counseling, acupuncture, chiropractic and other healthcare professionals.

4. Have established a part-time business but want to grow it to a full-time income.

You might be a student in one or more of these modalities. You could be a practitioner who has been in business for a couple of years, yet your business struggles to maintain a full-time reliable income. You could be operating an existing practice that is doing well, yet the idea of self-promotion, marketing and advertising is overwhelming.

When it comes to your practice, what keeps you awake at night?

- Not enough clients/patients?
- Are your finances and budget a disaster?
- Are you stretched trying to juggle areas of the business that make no sense?
- Is admin paperwork and processing piling up?
- Has your family life or health been affected by the stress of running your own business?
- Have you looked in your toolkit and noticed necessary tools and resources are missing?
- Or maybe you have wondered whether it's worth continuing, perhaps contemplated a career change, even though you still have a passion for what you do.

Believe me when I say, you won't be the first or last practitioner to ponder these questions.

Fortunately for me, prior to training as a practitioner years ago, my business background was in Sales and Marketing, so that part of running a small business comes naturally for me. But it isn't that way for many of us.

I have been in business and practice as a clinical hypnotherapist/ mentor since 2006. It hasn't all been sunshine and rainbows but as a result of my marketing, sales and various admin adventures and misadventures, I have developed my business success formula for a thriving healthcare practice, and I am frequently asked to share the secret to my clinic success with other practitioners.

I love the work that I do. I have passion not only for my clients' success but also for the success of other practitioners. From personal experience, I know how to navigate the pitfalls of operating a small business while applying the marketing and sales skills to keep clients coming through the door.

Many people in the healing arts have done the therapeutic training, they also love helping others, but they are out of their comfort zone when it comes to juggling the sales, marketing, administration and business hats.

Juggling hats formula

In your mind I invite you to step out of your business for a moment and imagine that you are now the owner of four hats. Each hat is a 'player' in the business and wants a dividend.

Hat number 1: Employee of the business.
Hat number 2: Manager of the business.
Hat number 3: Owner of the business (the investor).
Hat number 4: You.

In effect, each of those players wants a return on their investment (R.O.I.).

1. The employee has given time and effort and wants a return via a wage.

    They want to be paid for the work that they have given to this business.

2. The manager of the business is also invested in the business.

    Even though the manager isn't seeing clients/patients face to face, they're still communicating with them. The manager of the business is responsible for making sure that the marketing (lead generation, lead conversion and customer fulfillment), advertising and promotion, and admin work has been delivered. They're also responsible for ensuring that the business is running to budget. It's an important role and if this hat doesn't fit well, then business results, cashflow and general work satisfaction will reflect that.

3. The owner of the business is the one who has risked the initial investment of time and money.

    They're the player who had the original dream. They want their R.O.I. too. Think of it as being the owner of shares or an investment portfolio. You have put the money and time in, and you want to know that everything and everyone is working to maximize the investment.

4. The fourth hat is YOU.

    This is where you bring your own personality and expertise to the business. It's also where you look for and require balance. You're an integral component of the business and yes, the dream can't happen without you.

> *The dream can't happen without the entire team of players.*

There have been times when I too wondered just what the hell was going on. I often thought in the early years of setting up my practice, "This was supposed to be a dream. I've done the training, I love helping people to make amazing changes, I'm good at what I do … so where are the clients?"

As I write this book, I can imagine many readers nodding their heads in agreement. We can agree, business can be challenging. But it doesn't have to be that way. When you get your business right, and the players feel supported by both systems and knowledge, the rewards can be endless.

According to the American Bureau of Labor Statistics, *20% of small businesses fail in the first year*. Let's have a fresh look and reframe that statistic.

It could also be said that 80% of small businesses are ready for business growth in their second year. It can be assumed that one of the major contributors to their success is that they had a plan and they made the time to prioritize the implementation of that plan.

Further statistics reveal that 90% of business start-ups fail.[1]

There is something to be said about the power of the dream that drives people to succeed in business. It is also worthwhile reflecting on the key reasons why start-up businesses have failed.

---

1   Griffiths, Erin, "Why startups fail, according to their founders", Fortune.com, September 25, 2014.

A recent study by CB Insights cited that:

- 42% of responders indicated a lack of market need for their product or service was to blame for their failure.

- Other prominent pointers were poor cash flow (29%).

- Lack of a business model (17%).

- Poor marketing (14%).

- Ignore customers (14%).

- Burn-out (8%). [2]

I've addressed these key reasons for failure in this book. If these are the main reasons that we, as small business owners (and therapists), are not coping or succeeding beyond that first year or two, it is my aim to provide you with the steps to manage and overcome these challenges.

I take the view that in business, and in life, if you don't have the answer and Dr Google can't help you, then find someone who either does have the answer or can help you to find the solution. This is a time to be working smarter, not harder. This is a time to be calling on extra resources for the help that you need. You haven't come this far in your business journey to throw in the towel. You don't want to be another statistic of a practitioner who spent thousands of dollars in training, only to find that they just couldn't survive in business. Operating a business is simply another skill. Don't walk away from the career you were passionate about "to get a real job," before you learn the right business survival skills first. Make a difference from the position of strength first.

What if the healthcare path that you have chosen is the "real job"? What if you could actually make it work and the business started to make sense? We can always turn the "what if" question into

---

2   Ibid., Griffiths, Erin.

a positive as it's too often couched as a negative. The business person who walks around covered with a permanent rain cloud might say, "What if this is as good as it gets?"

> *You could always respond with, "What if this is just the start of amazing things to come?"*

Disaster Planning and Management:

Wouldn't it be wonderful if we could apply a perfect timing principle to all of our business decisions? Just when I was about to send this book to the editor for final draft approval, we were beset with the Coronavirus (COVID-19) pandemic that has shaken societies and economies both locally and globally, in ways that no one living has ever experienced. Just when you thought being in business was already challenging, overnight it just got a whole lot tougher.

I can hear Gloria Gaynor's voice somewhere in the back of my mind singing "I Will Survive." I remained confident through the worst of the Covid-19 early months that I would survive in business, however I also knew to be ready to make quick changes and adapt to the new environment.

Those businesses that can adapt to change with new flexible practices are the ones who will still stand at the end of the COVID-19 lockdown and any other crisis the world may experience in years to come.

On reflection, the timing of this book being published couldn't have been better, it helped me pause and add an extra chapter to this book, as a guide to help you to "disaster proof" your business.

As this book goes to press now, I sit firmly on the other side of the worst that the pandemic could throw at a small healthcare business, and I learned much about pivoting a business and reinforcing your relationship with your patients and customers during extraordinary times like this. Whether the event is an economic downturn, bushfires, floods, a viral pandemic or an earthquake, you have to be ready to call upon your own resilience and flexibility to not only pull through but survive and thrive and remain *Fully Booked*. When you quickly adapt and read how to best serve your customer and the industry in times like this, you learn a great business skill for life.

So dear reader, let's have an open conversation about *your* business.

This is my promise to you. By the end of this book you will have clarity about:

- Who you are.
- What you offer.
- What your successful business looks like.
- Who your target market is.
- How to market to those new clients and attract them with confidence.
- The basics of business administration.
- Having a strategy for a healthy work and life balance.

You will know that you have a successful business.

The challenge

I challenge you to not only develop more confidence in business, but to thrive. Isn't that what you want?

All I ask is firstly, that you commit yourself to enter each chapter as if you were entering into a conversation. The people in that conversation are you, me, and every other resource that you need right now to be that business success that you once dreamed of.

Secondly, that you give a commitment that you will give your business your best shot. There are exercises in each chapter to help you apply new learnings. Please complete these exercises to ensure the success of your business.

Strap on your seatbelts and let's make success happen.

To your success!

Brett Cameron

CHAPTER 1

It all begins with a dream

> *"Dreams are the touchstones of our character"*
>
> ~ Henry David Thoreau

We all dream. To have an imagination is what defines us as humans. Some people process information visually, they find visualizing easy, while others are more kinesthetic i.e., they process information through an emotional or tactile connection.

Some people are auditory while others are effective "numbers and processes" people. It really doesn't matter how you process information; the most important thing is that you have the capacity to imagine. You have the ability to dream of a world or a situation that's different from your current reality.

The dream

I haven't ever met one healthcare practitioner who didn't enter their profession originally without having a dream. It might have been a dream to bring health and healing to others. It might have been to have a career that was within your control and one that you really enjoyed doing.

If you're like me, you had a dream of practicing in a modern clinic setting, with a steady stream of clients/patients and going home to a balanced family life, knowing that your bank balance was forever on the right side of the ledger.

"Nothing wrong with that dream," I hear you say. Never lose sight of that original dream. It's by refocusing on that original dream that we keep going in those quieter times of the year.

What is your dream?

What imagined future motivated you to take a leap of faith and become a member of the healing arts?

In this chapter we'll explore that dream, who you are, define your personal and business narrative, create your perfect client avatar, and then begin to look at researching your competitors so that the foundation of your dream can fully manifest.

Who are you?

At this moment, I want you to imagine that I am your coach and you are seeking to have an improved game in whatever you do. As your coach/mentor I'll begin by asking you a simple question. "Who are you?"

For many of my clients and mentees, it's one of the most difficult questions to answer. By answering this question, you're taking the first step towards creating your unique business identity.

It all begins with you

It's your business and your individuality that will propel that business forward.

Activity

Either in your mind or as a written exercise, ask yourself the following questions.

- What are your values?
- What defines you?
- Are there behaviors and habits you find annoying?
- Apart from business dreams, what life dreams do you have?
- What prevents you from achieving those dreams?
- If I was to talk with one of your best friends, how would they describe you?

This is a moment for you to stand in your truth, to tell your story so that not only do you feel confident when communicating with members of the public and your professional peers, but you also feel comfortable in your own skin.

Be honest. Stand in front of a mirror and proudly say out loud …

"My name is (insert name here), and I'm a professional (insert profession here)".

How does that feel? Does it feel authentic or is there a part of you that feels like a fraud? Is there a tail-end voice that doubts or hesitates?

If so, you wouldn't be the first or last person to have feelings of discomfort when doing the exercise. Throughout this book that discomfort will begin to transmute into a feeling of quiet confidence and self-belief.

(For extra activities and exercises, including the full 'Who Am I?' questionnaire, see the Maximum Benefits section at the end of this chapter.)

Define your story

This book is a discussion with you about you and your business, whether you're currently in business or just starting out. (For the sake of this discussion, I'm going to assume that you're either still studying in your chosen field or you are already in practice.)

Let's create the narrative of how you got to where you are now.

You might have had to overcome life challenges yet here you are. You might have been inspired to take this career path by a parent or a family member, or it might have been a long-held dream.

Your life could have been cruising along with no major blips on the radar and you reached a point where you wanted some deeper meaning with a different career choice. Many people get to a crossroads where their chosen career doesn't fulfill them anymore. They feel compelled to follow a dream. It doesn't matter what the path has been, what matters is that this is *your* path.

You've learned and developed amazing and dedicated therapeutic skills as a healthcare practitioner, yet at the end of the day, the simple fact remains you are also a business owner.

While we can retell with happiness and joy, the dreams that were realized, everyone has memories of having dreams that perhaps didn't eventuate how they'd hoped.

What dreams of yours have eventuated?

Dreams I have had that came true

THE DREAM	WHAT MADE THE DREAM COME TRUE?

What dreams of yours have never been realized?

Dreams I have had that didn't come true

THE DREAM	WHY WAS THE DREAM NEVER REALIZED?

I encourage you to question whether the dream has failed to materialize because it remained just a dream, without the application of a plan and actionable steps.

Another approach I often use is to apply the SMART Goal Setting formula to a dream.

There are variations on the SMART formula, but this is the one that works for me.

SMART

Specific	Is the goal specific or has it been worded as a wish?
Measurable	Can you measure the goal as an outcome?
Agreed	Is it agreed with a coach/mentor? What else do you need?
Realistic	Is it realistic? If not, the chances of failure increase.
Timely	Is the goal set against a timeframe, e.g. by the end of this year?

To make the goal achievement more watertight, I encourage clients to also add in the PURE and CLEAR acronyms as suggested by John Whitmore.[3]

---

3   Whitmore, John, Coaching for Performance, Nicholas Brealey Publishing, London, 2004, p.61

PURE

Positively Stated	Is the language moving towards rather than away from?
Understood	Is the language clear and not ambiguous?
Relevant	How relevant is the goal in the big picture?
Ethical	Is the goal ethical?

CLEAR

Challenging	Will this goal challenge you to grow?
Legal	Of course, you have no legal issues with this goal.
Environmentally sound	Does this goal help you in your business environment?
Appropriate	Is this goal appropriate for now?
Recorded	Have you recorded the goal rather than it remaining a thought?

Think of one business goal and see if you can describe it by the SMART principle.

_____

_____

_____

_____

Knowing the current resources that you have at your disposal (financial, time, skills, energy, beliefs etc.), give yourself a percentage rating of your ability to reach that goal.

If for example you nominate an 80% chance of success, then by working with a coach, their role would be to help you find the resources to fulfill the 20% that's missing.

Finding the crucial missing 20% is the step that will turn your dream into a goal, and that goal into reality. The missing 20% might have a limiting belief at its foundation that stops you from following through.

We'll be exploring limiting beliefs and how to overcome them more fully in Chapter 3.

Who are You?

I love the, "Who are you?" question as it's so open-ended.

> *The more layers of the artichoke that are peeled, the closer to the heart we find ourselves.*

Take stock of who you are. Getting to the core of YOU.

What core beliefs do you hold about success and failure?	1
	2
	3
	4
	5
Where else in your life have you enjoyed success?	
Describe your history of family business success, or is this all new?	
Were you encouraged to succeed or did you have your dreams and aspirations belittled by others?	

Give examples of how your resilience plays out in life?	
Will you be supported in your business by loved ones? Or is this a solo effort? Describe how this makes you feel.	
Do you consider yourself a control freak, or can you let go and entrust others with key components of your business?	
Describe your thoughts on whether you deserve to be successful?	
How will you change as a person when you are successful in business?	

These and many other questions about you as a person and as a business owner are important. You may wear a business hat, but underneath you are still you.

Failure and Success

In most people's minds, failure is not an option. Likewise, I have worked with clients who have a fear of success. It can be quite lonely when you succeed as you might be out there reaching new heights, while everything that you have known is "back there" in the safety zone.

I know of people in business and elite sport who have very successfully sabotaged their success so that they could skulk back into the comfort zone. Of course, they don't often do that consciously. However, if the unconscious mind is programmed to apply roadblocks when you step out of your comfort zone, then until that pattern is reprogrammed, the unconscious sabotage wins every time.

But that isn't you, is it? What measures will you take to ensure that you won't sabotage your success?

What, if any, are the fears that could hinder that desired success?

_____

_____

Do you have a fear of failure or a fear of success? If so, how does it manifest?

_____

_____

_____

In Chapter 3, I explore limiting beliefs and negative patterns, so these are questions I will tackle in great with you depth then.

Composing your business narrative: Communicating your dream

When you talk to a total stranger and they ask what you do for work, how comfortable do you feel when telling your story?

If the story doesn't flow, and you have levels of discomfort or hesitancy, then the narrative requires some work. If you find yourself "umming and ahhring" while stumbling for words, or you notice a part of your body starts to twitch or feel ill at ease, then of course something unconsciously is not quite aligned.

I have to admit that this paragraph has been written from experience, as the person stumbling over those words used to be me.

When I was studying to be a hypnotherapist, I sometimes felt myself stumble over the word hypnotherapist when I was talking with others. I was aware that I might have been lacking internal conviction.

What did I do to overcome that lapse in confidence? I mentioned this hesitancy to David Kennedy, my teacher and mentor. He helped me to restate my purpose and to work through any limiting beliefs I held. I took the time to establish clarity.

ACTIVITY

1. Make a list of the things that you do really well.

2. What challenge do clients predominantly book to see you for?

3. What challenge do people often get referred to you for?

4. Tell a story that is not about you. Describe a client who came to see you to relieve their extreme *(insert problem here)*. After seeing you they messaged back to express their thanks as the problem is now in the past.

5. What words would a trusted friend use to describe you? Put yourself in the third person and write down these value words.

6. Make a list of key phrases or words that you would use in casual conversation. If you are going to borrow other people's words, make sure that you rework them so that what you say sounds authentic. If you are telling a story and the words that you use aren't genuine, it will come across that way.

7. Rehearse your story. How did you come to work in the healthcare industry? What led you down this path? What was your original business dream? What is your business dream for the next five years?

8. Practice in front of a mirror and become aware of your body language. If there is any incongruence when telling your story, then change the words or tonality until it flows smoothly.

When I did these exercises regularly, my story began to feel and sound right, I would speak that story with passion daily, until I was energetically fired up. I'd practice again and again until the words and phrases flowed easily.

You have to learn the story until it becomes energized, until even your muscles know the story as your truth.

Defining your business

Starting out in business can be daunting, challenging, exciting, rewarding and in any one day, it could be all of that.

When starting in business most of us are keen and ready to put our stamp on the world. You complete your training and you are one step closer to making it a reality.

TIP

Cash reserves: Start a new business with at least six months cash reserves. If you plan to be working part-time as you have another job, you might only need three months cash reserve.

Clarity: let's outline your business

Consider your target market:

Your modality and product you offer	Your ideal client	Why will they choose you? What is unique about you or your practice?
Example: Weight loss program with hypnosis	Example: Women Aged 40-55 Approaching or going through menopause	Example: Local expert, offer follow up support system, have nutritional experience too, once had a weight challenge, so understand the client's story etc.

Think about two of your previous perfect clients; these should be two clients you really enjoyed working with.

Let's call these "My ideal clients" (1).

- What are their ages and genders?
- What are their other demographics?
- Why did they seek your services?
- What is it about your practice that attracted them to you?
- What are their likes and dislikes?
- How did they find you?
- What clubs, groups were they a part of?
- What social media did they use most?
- What did you like when working with them?

Once you are clear about that client avatar, that person should become the core focus of your marketing energy.

That ideal client is where you need to focus your energy to attract more of the same.

As a hypnotherapist, while I see people from all ages, demographics and walks of life, if I was to picture my perfect client, they are either male or female, aged 35-50, have achieved some life goals with education, career and family, yet the common challenge they face is that they have reached a stage in life where they are stuck. They might be experiencing underlying anxieties about their future.

My ideal client is in the "where to from here?" phase.

I love working with those clients because I seem to have a natural empathy with them and, at an unspoken level, they are drawn to me too.

Think about your next perfect client (2).

Even though they may not be your first preference ideal perfect client, you will soon find that they become your 'bread and butter' client who will have your practice fully booked.

- What is their demographic, age and gender?
- What is their typical malady that requires correction?
- Why have they chosen you?
- What is it about your practice that has attracted them?
- What clubs, groups were they a part of?
- What social media did they use most?
- What did you like about working with them?

Personally, I find it rewarding to work with clients who have been beset with anxiety/PTSD/panic attacks.

These clients make up over 50% of my client base. I also see clients for weight release, smoking cessation and a range of fears and phobias.

Some of those clients don't match my perfect client avatar, but because I focused my attention on my top (1) and (2) clients, rather than scattering my marketing energy everywhere, I fill my calendar with my ideal clients and then other clients with challenges outside of this scope find me anyway.

You are in practice and in business and you will attract the clients who have either been referred to you or have found something in your marketing or brand that speaks to them directly.

How do you attract your target market?

I'll cover this topic more in depth in Chapter 4, but for now it's important to assess what you currently do. This is where to start when putting your focus toward attracting clients.

Researching competitors:

Even before you start in business, you should spend considerable time and resources researching your potential market and your competitors.

I'm careful to use the word "competitors" instead of opposition. You will be, and are, competing with other businesses for a slice of the pie. You are not in opposition.

Competitive mindset

By adopting a competitive mindset, you can learn a lot about your market from your competitors. I recommend openly speaking with them. If you respect their place in the market there may be the opportunity to share cross-referrals.

There have been many instances where I've referred a client to another hypnotherapist because either I was booked out, or I felt that they'd be a better fit with another hypnotherapist who specialized by working with clients with a specific challenge. It makes sense to develop relationships with your competitors, rather than seeing them as rivals vying for the same business.

When researching competitors, put yourself in the position of a potential client

When you put yourself in your prospective clients' shoes, what do you look for in a therapist to help you? Pull the websites apart with a fine-tooth comb as you are looking for hooks and key phrases that speak to you. Do they specialize in one particular area or have they taken a generalist approach?

What images are they using? Are those images enticing and professional? What is their website layout like? Is it easy to navigate or clunky? Do they have an easy to find "contact me" button on each page? Do they have their prices or packages on their websites?

Do your competitors advertise in local media, whether it be print, digital or radio?

I'm asking you to be ruthless in your assessment, checking for noticeable errors, then store that information away. Learn what "not to do", so you don't repeat that mistake.

If something a competitor does in their marketing or brand is perceived as successful, then explore it further. Imagine your logo and image in that same spot.

Without being labelled a stalker, check out the competitor's office and location.

Once again, have they made mistakes that you wouldn't want to repeat? Or are they doing great things that you want to emulate or improve upon? In effect you are building up in your mind your point of difference.

Why you? Why would someone choose you to help them?

I invite you to analyze you. What is unique about what you offer? What are your points of difference? (See table below)

What are your individual strengths?	
What areas hold your passion?	
What personal skills do you bring to the practice?	
Describe your workspace? The environment you bring your clients into.	
Are your clinic hours a point of difference?	

Are your pricing, packaging and rates unique?	
Is your location unique?	
Are you easily accessible?	
What else is unique about you? Your pre and post services?	

Download a FREE Template at

www.youfullybooked.com/resources

Chapter 1 in Summary:

Once you can establish your USPs (Unique Selling Points), you will now know where your time and energy should be focused for marketing. You have now:

- defined your dream
- defined your narrative
- defined your ideal client
- researched your competitors
- defined your point of difference as a professional healthcare practitioner

Now we can take the journey within you a little further as we bring your inner dreamer, inner critic and inner realist into alignment so that we can invite your inner coach into the fold. When we align these aspects of you, you can embrace your dreams and motivate yourself into action too.

Maximum Results Activities

For those of you who are action takers, and who seek fast and maximum results, complete the following activities.

Imagined Reality exercise

Close your eyes and realign with your business dream. Imagine you have the dials from an old-fashioned television set, you turn up the color and make the image compelling. Adjust the dials to bring the image into sharp focus. Ensure you are inside the scene looking out, feeling it, experiencing it with all your senses, not observing the scene, detached from the outside looking in. Replay this scene in your mind every morning when you wake.

Who am I? questionnaire

Complete this questionnaire to refine the person who will make your business a success. You!

What defines you? _____

_____

What makes you unique? _____

_____

What is it about you that makes you an individual? _____

_____

List five values that are rock solid ... you will never compromise these values for anyone or anything.

a. _____

b. _____

c. _____

d. _____

e. _____

To download a template of this questionnaire go to:

www.youfullybooked.com/resources

List five secondary values that are also important but flexible.

a. _____

b. _____

c. _____

d. _____

e. _____

List five traits, values or behaviors of your parents or a primary caregiver that you admire.

a. _____

b. _____

c. _____

d. _____

e. _____

List three achievements you're proud of, where you feel you were being true to yourself.

a. _____

b. _____

c. _____

List five traits, values or behaviors of loved ones, or work colleagues that you find annoying.

a. _____

b. _____

c. _____

d. _____

e. _____

Now is the time to dream ... list five things that in your wildest dreams you would love to do ... but you often think, "nah ... it's only a dream."

a. _____

b. _____

c. _____

d. _____

e. _____

List the things that stop you from realizing those dreams:

a. _____

b. _____

c. _____

d. _____

e. _____

List five people who you either know, would have liked to have known, or maybe they have a place in history that makes them admirable. Why are they on your list?

a. _____

b. _____

c. _____

d. _____

e. _____

Fast forward way into the future. You are on the verge of taking your last breath. You have the opportunity to write your own obituary. How would you like to be remembered? What are your life's golden achievements?

a. _____

b. _____

c. _____

d. _____

e. _____

My story: I want to share with you, the dream that I have for the first five years of the 2020s. I am also being mindful of the impact that COVID-19 has had on the economy.

If the planets remain aligned, and I remain in good health, and I stick to my business and marketing plans, there is no reason for me to not realize my dream.

My dream is to continue being a successful hypnotherapist in private practice being "Fully Booked".

I also mentor many other therapists around the globe as they move to become leaders in their field. I speak to many therapists internationally either in person, via my books, or through my online courses, helping those who are ready to become successful in their healthcare business.

My personal life is blessed with a fine balance of work, study, travel, gardening, swimming, listening to music, reading books and spending beautiful moments with my wife and family.

What is your dream? Take time to write down your five-year dream

_____

_____

_____

Remember you can download a FREE Template of the _Who Am I Questionnaire_ at:

www.youfullybooked.com/resources

In the following chapter, I let you in on one of the secrets that is at the foundation of my success in clinical practice. It's all about aligning your inner dreamer, inner critic (we all have one), your inner realist and your inner coach. Success happens when every part of you is on the same page.

CHAPTER 2

Align your inner dreamer, critic, realist and coach

> *"You just can't let nature run wild."*
>
> ~ Walt Disney

When I was a student of Neuro Linguistic Programming (NLP), one of the processes I loved was "Align the dreamer, realist and the critic".

This is a problem-solving mind process that was inspired by Walt Disney who, in the 1950s, would sometimes step in as the critic when his teams were developing projects. He would step into a project stating that there were three different Walts. There was the dreamer, the realist and the spoiler. No one knew which Walt was coming to the meeting.

His interventions were designed to rattle the cages of the dreamer and the realist to make sure that all avenues had been explored. In 1994, NLPer Robert Dilts, modified the Disney process and created Align the Dreamer, the Realist and the Critic NLP process.

For the purpose of this exercise, I've added the Inner Coach to the equation, because if we don't have innate inner support, humans tend to rely on external support for their motivation and stamina. I believe the inner coach is the final piece to the puzzle and provides us with self-regenerating motivation and stamina.

So, how does it work? I'll use the writing and publishing of this book as an example. To make this book a reality I had to do some internal realigning.

Internal Elements	What did they say about the idea of writing a book?
The Dreamer	The Dreamer loves the idea of writing a book. He has a vision of the book being a global best seller, helping many thousands of healthcare practitioners to pave their life path with gold and personal achievement.
The Critic	The Critic said, "Are you kidding me? You've never written a book. You won't know where to start, how to publish it or how to market it. In fact, it won't happen."
The Realist	The Realist said, "Hang on a minute. If we can gather the right resources and speak with the right people, and look at this from a different perspective, we can make this work."
The Coach	At this point I had to engage a coach (both external and internal) to pull all of these conflicting forces together. The coach is the one who develops strategies and continually checks in with the dreamer, the critic and the realist to make sure that they are on board.

Now it is your turn. Think of a dream that you have for your business. Get the picture clear in your mind by bringing in all the senses. Magnify the senses and make the picture as beautiful as you can. See it, feel it, touch it, smell it, hear it. It is your dream.

Internal Elements	What is the dream? How is it perceived?
The Dreamer	
The Critic	
The Realist	
The Coach	

The process works best when you keep bouncing the idea around between the internal elements until they are all in agreement.

Ultimately, the Inner Critic has to be satisfied that this project can be completed. Be aware that:

- The Dreamer will always think it can work.
- The Realist, if given the right tools and resources, will make it happen.

To download Your Dream Template go to:

www.youfullybooked.com/resources

- It's then the job of the Inner Coach to bring this project to fruition, to stay on track, motivate, seek help when needed and call upon the other parts of you to help, e.g. the inspiring part, the creative part and so on.
- If the Inner Coach needs help, then it will motivate you to seek help from an external Coach.

Don't be alarmed if this process goes around in circles. If that's the case, then there's a part of you that still needs to be convinced. Don't give up just because the process is still germinating. Allow the cycle to continue until you resolve the inner critic's doubts, judgments or concerns.

I was discussing the effects of the Disney process with Laureli Blyth. Laureli is a world leading NLP trainer based in Sydney, Australia. She told me about a "spacial" process she uses when turning developing ideas into practical realities.

Laureli made three spacial places using the Disney model. She would use her dining room table at home and a break table at work to be the dreamer. This is where she would let herself really look into the unlimited possibilities and big picture of what she wanted to do or achieve. She would take this back to her desk and computer to the realist position. This is where she does the planning and puts together the practical applications and work.

From time to time she would stop and take the practical work to a special chair in her house and special chair at work, to study it from a Meta position, or observer or the critic position. This is without emotional attachments. There you can give yourself feedback on what is working well and what might need to be cut or added later or added now. This allows her to go back and dream more if she wishes or she can take it back to the realist and make adjustments. Keeping these three spacial areas separate has provided clear, concise and practical, yet amazing, results. Laureli has used this method to help her write several books and workshops, created another successful business and much, much more.

Another process that complements the dreamer-critic-realist-coach work is The Three Brain Theory.

I encourage clients to embrace this theory at any time that a major decision needs to be made.

The Three Brain Theory

When confronted with a major decision, ask yourself three important questions.

- What does my head brain think?
- What does my heart brain feel?
- What is my gut brain telling me?

Imagine for a moment that the three brains are all contributing elements to the creation of a beautiful orchestra. Each component has a vital role to play. If any part of the orchestra is playing out of tune, then the symphony fails miserably.

There is no such thing as hindsight when making a business decision.

Your head brain

Is the thinking brain. It's applying logic and is developing strategies to help you in the decision process.

Your heart brain

Is the feeling brain. It's engaging feelings and emotions so that you can connect with the world.

The gut brain

Is the intuitive brain. It's asking you to follow your instincts and intuition. It's vital to consult the gut brain in this process because it knows you, as it's connecting with your sense of identity.

The Three Brain Process

Think of a business decision that you have had to make, e.g. you might have been inspecting a potential office space for a new practice.

The office space is a shop front on a busy street, positioned alongside mixed retail businesses. Parking availability is limited to street parking. You decide to sign a lease, as you're desperate to get your business up and running. Six months later, the practice isn't as busy as you'd hoped and you're under financial pressures. Let's ask the three brains for some input.

The head brain will answer:

"Well you didn't consult me. If you had asked me for an opinion, I would have said you can't afford it. I also would have told you that as it was impossible to find a park when you inspected the office, where did you expect your clients to park?"

The heart brain will answer: (which was the only brain that was initially consulted)

"I love this office. The retailers are busy and there's consistent foot traffic in the street. You love coffee, and there's that funky café next door. This area just feels so good."

The gut brain will answer:

"If you had thought to trust in my judgment, I would have given you so many reasons as to why this wouldn't be a good move. Remember the graffiti on the front wall, and the constant wailing of fire engine sirens from the fire station across the road? It just didn't feel right."

You have to weigh up all the competing thoughts and emotions in order to make a decision that will bring rewards. In utilizing the three-brain theory, if you don't get three ticks of approval, one from each brain, then don't do it.

> *If the thinking brain, the feeling brain and the intuitive brain have all been engaged equally, and they all agree, then the end result will be a finely-tuned orchestra producing a harmonious symphony.*

I had a dream, yet I failed: Business people who bounced back

> *"If at first you don't succeed, then try, try again"*
>
> ~ Thomas H. Palmer

There are many statistics about businesses that have failed. You started with a dream and everything was going in the right direction, and then bang! The wheels fell off the business and you were going nowhere fast.

When confronted with defeat, it's only those who can call on reserves of courage and resilience who survive.

In the world of business, (yes remember, you are in business,) there have been many before you who are now at the top of the business tree, yet they will all tell you of a tale of initial business failure.

1. "You are too old to start your own business". Tell that to a young 56-year-old **Colonel Harland David Sanders** who had a dream of starting a chain of chicken restaurants. His recipe for his now famous Kentucky Fried Chicken was reportedly rejected up to 1,000 times until success knocked on his door.

2. "Your ideas won't work ... you lack imagination." Imagine if **Walt Disney** had listened to the newspaper editor, put his tail between his legs and disappeared into the sunset. Instead Disney World is valued at over US$130 billion. (April 2019)

3. "When I was on the floor, curled up in that little ball, I seriously considered giving up, going back to my old life and getting a job, at that stage I wanted something easy. But I refused to give up. In the years after the gala we went on to raise over $3.5 million and support the education of more than 10,000 women and girls." ~ **Chantelle Baxter** from Be.Bangles. Chantelle talks about planning a fundraiser for six months and when the event rolled around, she had raised only one fifth of her charity target, but perseverance and a little luck (yes, we sometimes need luck) paid off.

How will you align your inner dreamer, critic, realist and coach so that you don't have to just learn from failings, but instead grow and learn from success too?

My story

Casting my mind back to 2005, I was ready to jump off the corporate tiger, strap on a pair of "I'm going into business" wings and prepare to jump off a cliff.

All of this was in the hope that I would somehow learn to fly before I hit the ground. Oh, the joy and wonderment of hindsight! I was living and working in Sydney, Australia for an international company in the homeware's industry. I had gained experience as a Training Manager, and then as a National Sales Manager, I managed a team of salespeople.

But I had no previous experience of being my own boss. To throw a hand grenade into the mix, my wife had just been diagnosed with Motor Neuron Disease (MND) (known as ALS in the United States), and she was given a life expectancy of two years. No stress!

In essence, we had both jumped out of our respective career planes, and neither of us had a parachute. Cynthia was determined to beat this dastardly disease and she devoted her time to healing, while at the same time seeing clients in our new hypnotherapy practice. My previously stable roles had changed overnight as well.

Did I align my dreamer, critic, realist and inner coach? No

Did I apply the magic of the Three Brain Theory? No

Why not? Because at the time, I was arrogant, bulletproof and foolhardy. And scared!

I wouldn't have admitted that at the time because as far as I was concerned, the world was waiting for me. Thankfully, through all of the bounces along the runway of business life, I finally learned how to get off the ground.

If I had applied my more mature and learned voice to that younger upstart, it might have sounded something like the following:

Internal Elements	What is the dream? How is it perceived?
The Dreamer	I have a dream of having a Fully Booked clinical hypnotherapy practice where I have a perfectly balanced business, family and creative life with a comfortable income.
The Critic	You must be joking. The only business experience you have is when you tried to help your father out of his business failings. Have a look at what happened to him. Do you want to repeat that?
The Realist	If you can develop a professional business structure, and engage the right mix of experts, then you have the intellect and drive to make a business succeed.
The Coach	Make a list of areas where you require help and I'll help find those resources. I'll speak with the critic and the realist to get them on board, and we might have to adjust the dream a bit as we learn.

Likewise, if I had applied the Three Brain Theory at that time the conversation could have been as follows:

The head brain	I'm only on board if you get some serious business advice and guidance.
The heart brain	I love this. This business is going to fly. I'm passionate and that passion alone will get us through.
The gut brain	Oh, I don't know about this idea of yours. My gut is in knots just knowing what can possibly go wrong.

Chapter 2 in Summary:

I designed this chapter as an opportunity to explore the inner components of you.

You can always have a dream of where your business should be, but if you haven't reached an agreement with the four inner components of you, then you'll continue to sabotage that success, and nothing will ever be achieved.

By adding the neurological systems of the Three Brain Theory you now have positive tools to take you forward. You have:

- Learned to align the dreamer, the inner critic, the realist and the inner coach.
- Developed an understanding of the Three Brain Theory.

You have examples of how to use both systems to align the parts of you onto the same page (the same dream).

In the following chapter, it's time to take off the dreamer's hat and face the nasty old negative patterns that in the past have held you back. Let's address that little nagging voice in the back of your mind that puts you down, doubts every forward step and focuses your mind on "what if I fail?" instead of "what if I succeed?"

Let's talk to that little part of you, expose it, and give it a new positive role before we delve into business strategy and planning. If we don't attempt to address it here, the strategy and planning will be to no avail later.

TIP

When handing a business card to a client, always give them two. Ask them to hand one card to someone who they know would benefit from your services.

CHAPTER 3

Freedom from limiting beliefs and old negative patterns

> *"We ought to relentlessly ignore excuses, especially those we are told by ourselves."*
>
> ~ Mokokoma Mokhonoana

Let's open this conversation and talk more about the most important element in your business ... you.

It never ceases to amaze me, the number of times I will be in conversation with a struggling practitioner and we come to the realization that it is they themselves who are holding the business back from further success.

Let's start from the premise that you have entered into business with a vision in mind of how you and the business will look and how it will be structured.

Actually, I'll correct that last sentence. I *hope* that you have entered into business with a vision in mind of how your business will look and how it will be structured.

It's a time when emotions bump along on extreme highs and lows. I know that when I started seeing clients in my hypnotherapy practice, I was caught in an unknown world, where I wanted to see and work with everyone, yet my lack of confidence in some areas held me back. I was keen to grow my practice, yet there was an unspoken hesitancy that slowed my progress.

A limiting belief is something that you consciously or unconsciously believe to be true, and by holding on to that belief, you remain stuck.

That belief might appear to the analytical brain to be totally ludicrous, yet the emotional brain says, "It's been with me for so long it must be true." In time, that belief will start to impact upon your behavior.

Behavior is organized around beliefs. If you believe in something, then your behavior will reflect that belief. [4]

It's the reason why consciously I wanted to be successful in business, yet there was an unconscious belief that I'll follow my father's footsteps of business failure.

I've had many clients presenting with limiting beliefs and mental obstacles which they've battled for years. Some examples that other practitioners have shared with me are:

Belief 1:

"My father and his father had chronic back pain, and if I continue to play tennis I will also develop chronic pain." The massage therapist soon found out that both the father and grandfather were builder's laborers for most of their lives while the client was an accountant. Yet the client had an irrational belief that he was destined to have chronic back pain.

---

4   Bandler, Richard, Using Your Brain for a Change, Real People Press, Utah, 1985, p. 103.

Belief 2:

An overweight client was convinced that since most of her family were overweight, then she would inherit the family's "fat gene". She was also told as a child by her father, "Once a fatty, always a fatty". Now she was living that limiting belief.

Belief 3:

A client once told me, "My family are from the wrong side of the tracks. We've never had money. When I was younger, my religious grandmother used to tell me that our family were being punished by God for wasting money." The client had an unqualified belief that he, and their family, didn't deserve money.

Beliefs are the principles that guide actions

A business owner will have a set of principles that he or she acts upon, and also a set of values that they hold that determine the culture of the business.

What beliefs have the potential to prevent you from succeeding in business? Do we need to change any of those beliefs? Is it you? Do you have to get "you" out of the way?

What are your limiting beliefs? Test yourself with the following activity. You might be surprised at what you find. Consider what your limiting beliefs are and ponder the origin and what you intend to change (or not).

Limiting Belief	Where did it originate? Is it yours? How does it affect your business?	What will you do about it?

I had a conversation with English hypnotherapist Freddy Jacquin, and asked him what he does with clients presenting with limiting beliefs. He said, "We are all what we believe we are, yet that belief is rarely true".

Freddy suggested that once we understand that nothing exists outside of our skull except as perception, including beliefs, emotions, negative and positive thoughts and even physical pain, then we can decide how and what we want to believe, feel and experience.

Once we understand this, we can make a simple judgment on any belief that we hold; does this belief empower me or disempower me? Then if the answer is that the belief that you hold is disempowering you, you can choose to believe something else, because none of your beliefs are anything more than chemical: neurons and electrically excitable cells firing off in your brain. The same goes for our emotions and feelings.

In most cases the limiting belief exists as a protective device to make you feel safe. Freddy encourages the use of "parts negotiation" to find what the limiting belief is about, find its positive intention, and ask the unconscious mind to reassign that positive intention.

When is the right time for a price increase? What am I worth?

I know that in my city, the prices I charge for my services are the highest in the area for a hypnotherapist. I haven't always been that way, but I am now. I have no time to think about what others are doing.

If you are priced too low, then you might be attracting a demographic that is chasing the cheapest deal. The mindset of that client could be focused on pay a low dollar, get a service, and if the client doesn't feel that they benefited from the work, they can blame the practitioner. That client doesn't have any investment in the service that you have given. So, when is the right time for a price increase?

A friend told me a story about a busy restaurateur. His restaurant was always full of diners. His restaurant was so popular that people would line up outside in all-weather just waiting for a table.

While at the same time the restaurant next door was struggling. It was always mostly empty. The successful restaurateur spoke to a business friend asking his advice. The successful restaurateur asked, "Should I buy out the unsuccessful neighbor so I can expand my business? I can imagine having a larger space full of happy customers".

His business friend replied quite simply, "Put your prices up".

Remember always that when in business, you are beholden to the market. If you're too low in the price that you charge, your business mix and profitability will reflect that. Conversely, if you are overpriced, then you might be struggling to attract the right clientele who are prepared to pay a premium. It's a juggling act, yet if you trust your business intuition, you will know where to position yourself. Remind yourself that if you had a 10% price increase and this resulted in a 10% reduction in your number of clients, you will have the same income while doing less face-to-face work. Conversely, if the number of clients you see doesn't diminish, then perhaps you've found the right "sweet spot" for your pricing.

My Limiting Belief Story:

I was in a room with other budding authors, while my business coach and mentor, Maggie Wilde took us through a mind exercise to clear limiting beliefs or roadblocks that might have prevented me from writing this book.

I don't know where it came from, but I was suddenly emotional.

The words that came to mind and out of my mouth were, "I am not my father!"

Wow. That was a biggie. Maybe somewhere in the back of my mind I had held the subconscious belief that since my father had failed at business, then I must have been destined to repeat the family trait.

Yet I also know that another part of me balances that belief knowing that I am successful. By allowing that unconscious belief to surface, I no longer consciously nor unconsciously allow it to impact my life.

Now I have a belief that allows success in writing and digital marketing. It's not a fairy-tale but the short story ends with me overcoming the limiting beliefs, writing this book, being a published author and now you get to read and benefit from that shift and this book.

Chapter 3 in Summary:

If you have identified limiting beliefs and negative patterns that hold you and your business back, then you now have a great starting point for your next meeting with your business mentor or coach. Heal thyself.

In Chapter 4, I address your personal signature. This is the brand that aligns you with your prospective audience and customers. Let's get you branded … in a figurative sense.

CHAPTER 4

Standing out from the crowd

"Don't run with the crowd, fly with the stars."

~ Matshona Dhliwayo

How do you stand out from the crowd? What is your personal signature? This is the time to step back and have a fresh assessment of you as a brand. Put on your marketing hat and think of you and the work that you do, as a brand.

In this chapter, I'm asking you to explore what it is that makes you different. Remembering that first impressions are lasting impressions; you want to make sure that the message is clear every time. You also want to ensure that the message is you. While it's common practice to check out what others are doing for their marketing and branding as you look for inspiration, be mindful that once you have locked in your brand image, it's yours and should be a true reflection of you. You are original and so is your business.

1. Name of Business.

2. Branding: Design of logo and business image.

3. The brief for the Graphic Designer.

4. Office layout.

5. Consistent communication. How do I reach you?

6. Websites and Social Media: Attracting the target market.

What is the name of your business?

That's a tough question for many, while for others it just flashes into their minds. If you're flying solo, you might consider that your name can be incorporated into the name of your business, but it can be more than that. When I chose Cameron Hypnotics as my brand and business name, I went through many different options before the decision was made. I chose to link my surname with the work that I do, with a slight twist. I am a hypnotherapist and I do hypnosis and hypnotherapy. What is hypnotics? It's just a marketing twist on hypnosis.

When I finally decided on that business name, I asked myself several questions as I wanted to make sure I felt comfortable answering the phone with, "Thanks for calling Cameron Hypnotics, Brett speaking. How can I help you?" If it didn't roll off my tongue with ease, or I noticed a shoulder movement or physical discomfort when saying the words, then I would have known it wasn't the right name.

When it comes to deciding on your business name, consider your own name, your location, the modality that you specialize in, and what it is that sets you apart. When you have a short list of business names, do a poll with people whose opinions you respect. They could be close friends, family or business associates. The trick is to get out of your own way and not be offended if the majority votes for a name that you didn't have as your favorite. Always remember, the market always wins. This is also a good process when choosing colors, logo or anything that you're presenting to potential clients. If choosing a location as a part of your business name, be mindful that down the track, when you expand your business, you might have created an invisible obstacle.

It's important that your business name is available as a URL. I'd hate to think you'd go to all the trouble of creating a business name and brand, only to find out that someone else has registered that name. Be mindful of where you are in the world of business. If you are in the USA then it makes perfect sense to have a .com URL. However, if your business is in Australia and you are only promoting yourself to an Australian audience, then you would be registering your business as a .com.au URL.

ACTIVITY

1. Business name: Come up with three possible business names that work for you.

2. Poll your friends, family or respected peers.

3. Is the name available as a URL? You want to be able to lock it in as your web address. If you're outside the United States, and your business won't have an international audience, then don't go with a .com URL. It's best to stick with your country's code, e.g. Australia .com.au, New Zealand .co.nz, Canada .com.ca

4. What colors represent you, your business, and can be clearly identified as being "you"?

5. Get a graphic designer on board. You're a professional and you want to present a professional image at every step. If you can't find a local designer to fit your brief, put your work out to tender with designer platforms. It's not expensive and you might be pleasantly surprised at the results. Some examples of freelance designer platforms are:

www.upwork.com
www.fiverr.com
www.freelancer.com

TIP

Be clear when briefing your graphic designer. They will invariably charge you for time spent on your design, so if you don't communicate well on the original briefing, then you might be wasting money going back and forward to get to the final design. I know this from experience. For a start-up business I'd be requesting the following design suite.

A Briefing for your Graphic Designer:

1. Logo in full color and also black and white (ask for the RGB colors).

2. Logo in jpeg, .png in high and low resolution.

3. Business card layout. Personally, I value my business card, as I want it to represent me when I am handing it to a client. Think about what you want on the front and back. Some people want to have their photo on the card, however, that's something I wouldn't do. On the front of my card I have my logo, which is my business name. On the back I have my name and contact details and a space to write a client's next appointment date and time.

4. A web banner for your website.

5. A Facebook banner for your Facebook business page.

That's all you will need to start. Once you have the basics you're free to start creating flyers, letterheads and any internal personalized stationery. If you aren't already using a DIY designer website, it's time to start experimenting. Just do a search for "Graphic Design software" and you'll find a suite that's right for you. I've been using www.canva.com. There are many others available, so have a search and play around with the free versions before you commit. You don't have to be a graphic design maestro. There are loads of templates ready for you to change the color and the wording, insert your logo and then post to your website, favorite social media or marketing platform.

Branding? Logo? Colors?

What is the consistent image that represents you and your message to the public? This is your moment to stand out from the crowd and leave a clear and lasting impression on your potential client. I asked Jason Gemenis, a design industry expert, what tips he would give a start-up when looking at logo development. He said, "A logo is how you introduce your business to the world. A logo is more than just a mark that represents your business, though; it's the essence of your brand. It has a massive impact on the perception of your business, so it's crucial to create the perfect logo design for your business."

TIP

Always get appointment confirmations from your clients. They will know that you are prepared for them, and secondly nobody wants a "no show".

JASON HAS FIVE SIMPLE TIPS FOR LOGO CREATION:

1. Keep it simple: use no more than two colors and try not to use more than two fonts, with one being ideal, unless you have a monogram or slogan. Another way to keep your design simple is to use creative flourishes with caution.

2. Make it memorable: An effective logo uses an uncomplicated but punchy design. It stands out by using a bold font or an easy to remember shape.

3. Test for versatility: An effective logo should look good across a variety of platforms, both online and in print. To test your design, ask yourself a few questions:

   iv. Does this logo look good in one color?

   v. Can it be used in a space as small as a business card or as large as a billboard?

   vi. Can it be used in reverse, white on a black background or vice versa?

4. Ask, is it appropriate? Do your research and know what kinds of colors and fonts are good for your industry and what attracts your customers. It's not only about what you like.

5. Create for the long term: If you want a timeless logo, be sure to subtract everything that feels flashy or extra, you'll thank yourself later.

Branding is not a colorful logo and a bi-line. Branding is the set of values that are placed on your name and identity. When creating your own brand, the first question you have to ask yourself is, "How do I want to be perceived by the market?" What values do you want to be associated with your business? When I looked at my brand and how I wanted to consistently present that brand I looked at:

a. My promise: I want to be professional, fun, ethical, sincere, and to be seen as a leader of my profession.

b. All forms of communication. That includes verbal, digital, print, and even body language. My communication style has to be inviting, open, informative, consistent, and coming from a place of recognized authority.

c. Consistent visual message so that my logo is prominent but not dominant.

d. How my office reflects who I am, but I also want to give the client a quick understanding of what they can expect.

Does your office environment reflect your business?

When I was starting out as a hypnotherapist, I remember cringing when a weight loss client was describing another hypnotherapist they had previously seen. That hypnotherapist was working from a home office. (There's nothing wrong with working from a home office, as I still do. That office set up however, must be a reflection of your level of professionalism and must meet clients' expectations.) The client was guided through the therapist's house to his office, however the therapist's overweight family were sitting around the table eating pizzas as the client had to maneuver their way to the therapy room. Obviously, the client wasn't filled with confidence, as that hypnotherapist seemed to tick every box of "what not to do".

Does your office reflect who you are? Will a client feel comfortable and confident? I'm not suggesting that you get an interior designer to create a state-of-the-art working space. The client room has to reflect you and what you represent. Are the colors welcoming? Is the entrance clear? Do you have clean toilet facilities? If you are working from a home office, is the room separate from the house or family living areas? If you are in a shared office or clinic, is your area clearly defined as your work space? More importantly what is the client's immediate reaction when they walk into the room? First impressions can determine the outcome of the session.

Websites, Facebook Business Page, Instagram, Google my Business, Linkedin:

If you are in business or readying yourself to go into business, and you are weighing up the pros and cons of having a website, then read the next sentence and stop deliberating: GET YOURSELF A WEBSITE! Now how easy was that decision? To be in business and not have a website, is like having a random house with no house number, in a random street with no name, and you still wonder why you don't get any mail or visitors. No one knows you live there.

Website Brief:

How much does a website cost? How long is a piece of string? There are some amazingly complex websites and there are also some beautiful, sharp and concise websites that get the desired message across, give the reader as much information as they require to make a decision, and have a "call to action" button that prompts the user to make contact. Of course, there are also websites that give you every reason why NOT to support that business. When contacting a web developer, they'll ask you for a brief. That brief should contain:

1. Information about your business. This will be a summary about what you do, how you identify your brand, your history and values, and the products and services you offer.

2. What is your target audience?

3. What is the goal for the website?

4. Do you have a list of websites that you like and dislike?

5. Do you have an idea of how many pages and what the content will be?

6. Are you supplying content and images?

7. What is the deadline? When do you want the website to be live?

8. Hosting? Do you want them to host your website and mail server?

9. Budget? Yes that is important.

When I was ready to brief my web developer in late 2018 about my need for a new and fresh website, I was fortunate to have had a well-established working relationship with them as they had built my first website and were my existing web and mail host. The most important tips I have are:

1. Have a graphic designer on board to create web banners, logos, preferred font and typeface, and have your corporate colors established.

2. Be prepared to supply a library of images that reflect you and your business message. You will find many low cost online libraries, e.g. iStockphoto, Fotolia, Shutterstock and Pexels, to name a few.

3. Research web templates. I chose a Wordpress template that meant after the website was complete, I could go into the back end of the website, with administration rights,

and make any changes that I wanted, e.g. adding blogs and articles or changing images. You have to ask for administration rights.

4. Have a working relationship with the person who is actually building your website. If you aren't given that access, then you will have an increased chance of having a finished product that doesn't reflect you or your business.

5. Have a Google Analytics account so that you can track the performance of components of the website. This allows you to tweak pages and articles to maximize access to your website. You don't want to have a piece of art as your website that no one visits.

SEO? Is it all a mystery to you?

I've spoken to many healthcare practitioners who admit openly that they have no idea about SEO and how it affects their website. If you don't already know, SEO is Search Engine Optimization - it's the process of getting organic traffic to your website. It can be a very confusing topic. You should understand though that every website needs SEO. I asked my web developer, Melanie Morschel, to explain why we need effective SEO.

HERE ARE MELANIE'S FIVE BASIC SEO TIPS:

1. Carry out keyword research. If you don't know what your target market is searching for, how do you know what keywords you should optimize your website for? There are some great free tools available, such as Ubersuggest.

2. If you're building a new website, make sure your web developer incorporates SEO into the build at the beginning. Attempting to optimize later can be time consuming and expensive.

3. Backlinks are very important! Also called inbound links, these are links from other websites to your website. They represent a vote of confidence from one site to another and show the search engines that your website is important. Some backlinks are more valuable than others - quality is definitely better than quantity. This can be achieved by writing articles and blogs that might be of interest to other websites. You can also get links from businesses that you already support. It could be a case of, "I scratch your back, and you scratch mine." In essence you are helping search engines to find relevant content and links.

4. Understand the difference between on-page and off-page SEO. On-page SEO refers to the factors you can control on your website and incorporates aspects such as: using keywords in your copy, optimizing meta descriptions, writing SEO titles, using heading tags, and alt tags on your images. Off-page SEO refers to ranking factors that happen off your website, and includes backlinks, brand mentions, domain authority, and social networking.

5. The search engines want to see quality content. Simply building a website is no longer enough - your website needs to grow and change in order for it to be reindexed regularly. There's a variety of ways you can create new content - blogs, case studies, testimonials, and video.

FB Business Page, groups:

To have a business page on Facebook allows you to target your audience, locally and globally. Here are some no-brainer reasons why you must have a Facebook Business page:

1. Increase your exposure to attract more clients.
2. Lower your marketing and advertising expenses.
3. Reach a targeted audience instead of throwing the net wide in blind hope.
4. Use Facebook Insights to find out more about your client and your post.
5. Develop brand loyalty and recognition.
6. Increase your overall web traffic.
7. Increase your mobility as you have more access across all devices.

By joining or creating Facebook Groups, you are tightening the net. You now have a greater capacity to network with likeminded people, build customer relationships, and further build your brand. By being prominent in industry groups, you are also building your credibility as an industry leader and pace-setter.

Instagram:

In the competitive world of social media, Instagram has positioned itself in a visual format. It allows you to tell your story through images and videos, while Facebook, Twitter and Linkedin invite posts that combine text and image. The feel of Instagram is "light and fun." It gives you the opportunity to show a human side to your business by posting photos from your phone where you have added some short text. You are sending a person to person message to your potential market. You are not selling to your market, you are connecting.

If up to 60% of internet users between the ages of 18-29 have Instagram accounts, and that age group is your target market, then it makes sense to promote your business on Instagram. Instagram is owned by Facebook. You can link your Facebook and Instagram accounts so that any Instagram feed can appear on your Facebook page.

Almost 80% of Instagram users will follow businesses on Instagram Stories.[5] Donna Moritz from Socially Sorted says that one third of the most viewed stories on Instagram are by businesses.

Google My Business:

I love Google My Business. If you love Google then of course that love might be reciprocated. Google My Business is great for building your local SEO as it helps searchers to find local businesses and service. The benefits are many:

- It's free.
- You have a personalized page with your articles and blogs.
- It's a place to ask clients to leave Google reviews.
- You can track website traffic and audience.
- It helps clients find your location by placing you on a Google map.

---

5   https://sociallysorted.com.au/7-reasons-why-i-love-instagram/

Linkedin:

If Linkedin has over 660 million users around the world, then you should have your business listed there. The benefits are endless. Linkedin is another link in your branding chain. Linkedin marketing is about:

- Making connections.
- Generating leads.
- Fostering business partnerships.
- Sharing content.
- Driving people to your website.[6]

I take the view that Linkedin will have a different audience to other forms of social media. I have attracted many "business" clients from my Linkedin profile who would never be on Facebook or Instagram. My profile on Linkedin is different from my other profiles. I portray a more serious and business-like approach on Linkedin.

Consistent Communication: How do I Reach You?

Call to Action: There is a simple message in this paragraph. That message is to make sure that your contact details are on every piece of paper that has the potential to be seen by a prospective client. Make sure your contact details are on every page of your website. More importantly, ensure that you have a call to action, encouraging people to "click here to contact me". Even when researching this book, it was frustrating to look up someone who I wanted to contact as a reference, only to find that their website was a labyrinth that took me into many dark corners, but not to a contact page.

---

6   https://blog.hubspot.com/blog/tabid/6307/bid/23454/the-ultimate-cheat-sheet-for-mastering-linkedin.aspx

Phone message: Do you have a recorded message for the times when you can't answer the phone? Does it actually have a message? I recall phoning a fellow hypnotherapist and the phone call went to voicemail. The message said, "Leave a message". That was it. It didn't say, "Thank you for calling Xyz Hypnotherapy, I could be with a client or on the phone. Please leave a message with your name and a contact phone number and I promise I will call you back promptly." My first thought when I heard the abrupt message was, "How is this person in business?"

Messaging Service: There are arguments for and against the use of a third party messaging service. Yes, the client is talking with a human who takes the message. However, you are then reliant on that message being transferred to you accurately and in a timely manner. The message service cannot answer any questions about your service. Personally, it's a service that doesn't suit my business style; however it might work perfectly well for yours. The jury is still out on this one.

Stationery: The creation of consistent stationery is another step in the cementing of your brand in the minds of the client and broader market.

a. Business Card: Be mindful of the image that you want to portray. In some cultures, by presenting your business card to someone, you are in fact giving them a piece of you. There's an honor as the card has your name, logo and contact details. A personal hatred of mine, and please tolerate me on this one, is that I hate cheap and free business cards. My card is presented in landscape format with my logo on the front and contact details on the reverse. The card is professionally printed with a matte laminated finish.

b. Letterhead and office stationery: Consistency is the name of the game. You now have your logo and business name, so now is the time to use them. Every piece of paper that I print for the business has my logo on it: letterheads, flyers, client handouts, client intake forms, client questionnaires and bookmarks. Anything that has the potential to be seen by the client will have my logo in a prominent position.

My Story:

I'll be the first to admit that I am not a graphic designer. Yet I love to tinker with design software to create images that work for my business. I now have an idea of what my market likes and expects from me. It's a mixture of serious and fun, informative and light, yet usually on theme. It wasn't always that way. In 2012, I had a perfect storm of life changing events. Those events culminated in me moving back to my hometown of Newcastle, Australia. It was also the time that I gave myself permission to reinvent myself in business. My previous business name which I shudder when I think of it ... ok dear reader ... promise you won't laugh at me ... it was Channelled Growth. Yes, there was a time when I must have thought it made sense. Change towns, change business. I created the brand Cameron Hypnotics and, with it, I had a firm idea in mind of what that brand would look like and how it would be perceived.

Everything that I add to social media or to my website has to reflect the image that I am proud to put my name to. Every time I advertise or write an article, I'm aware of the colors and positioning of my logo, and what impressions the reader or potential market will have. Marketing is communicating. The trick is to know who you are, who your client is, and to what they want.

Chapter 4 in Summary:

This chapter has helped to identify how you can stand out from the crowd. Your business story is coming together.

1. Name of Business.

2. The brief for the Graphic Designer.

3. Branding: Design of logo and business image.

4. Websites and Social Media.

5. Office layout.

6. Consistent communication. How do I reach you?

Now we enter the part of the book that covers the key areas of why small businesses fail. I'm asking you to close your eyes, roll them around a bit, shake your shoulders, and begin to engage another part of your brain. Let's get your brain's left side on board as we have some business planning to do.

TIP

When choosing a CRM, do your homework. They can range from close to free to $100 per month or more. What do you need now, and is there flexibility for future growth?

CHAPTER 5

Business Success Starts with a Plan

"Those who fail to learn from the past are doomed to repeat it"

~ Winston Churchill

Okay, I have to sound a warning. The next couple of chapters are not the sexy chapters. These are the chapters where we cast aside the social media, marketing, logo, colors and branding fun side of the business. This is where we sit down and put on our serious business hat. I don't want to be the one who lets the air out of your balloon, but if you don't get the Business Plan and its implementation right, then the chances are good that you might be out of business before your dreams are realized. Now we don't want that to happen.

Have a look at the next three points, and ask yourself if they are in the correct order. How do you see yourself?

1. Business person?

2. Marketer?

3. Therapist?

I put this test to a healthcare practitioner who I'm mentoring and she responded by putting the therapist first. My answer was that if she sees herself as a therapist first and foremost, then she's not in business. Yes, you've done the training in your modality and you're probably very competent at what you do. However, you are now in business and marketing. That is how you have to position yourself mentally, emotionally and physically, or you will not survive. I can't make that point strongly enough.

If you don't take Chapters 5 and 6 seriously, then maybe you aren't taking your business seriously.

This is a time to try on different hats, but always ensuring that they suit you. You don't want to become another business failure statistic. Plan the development of your business by following a simple structure:

1. Business Plan: is a written description of the future of your business. It's a document that describes what you plan to do and how you plan to do it. [7]

2. Marketing Plan: is how you intend to market your product and service to the public. It will cover product mix, strategies, positioning and marketing goals. [8]

Business Plan Structure

1. **Executive summary:** An overall snapshot of the business. This will be a short, concise and positive overview of your business. The titles will include:

a. A mission statement telling the reader what your business will aim to do.

b. The company. Names of office holders and responsibilities.

c. A list of services offered.

d. Who is your target market?

---

7   https://www.entrepreneur.com/article/38290
8   https://www.businessknowhow.com/marketing/marketing-plan.htm

e. Financial projections for one year and three years.

f. Start-up finance requirements.

2. **Company/business description**: What do you do? This is the opportunity to go into greater depth, detailing your business goals.

3. **Office setup and environment**: Detailing how you visualize your office and workspace to be. The office is a reflection of you and your business.

4. **Marketing and Sales**: What products or services do you sell? How will you market them? This is an overview of the part of the business that will bring in the money. It's what you offer to the paying client. It is how you plan to structure that component.

5. **Market analysis**: Research market and competitors. Before launching into business, this is the moment to determine what will set you apart from every other practitioner in the market. Why will clients be attracted to you instead of other longer established practitioners?

6. **Financials and Licenses**: Develop a working budget (covered in greater detail in Chapter 6). Your financials will include forward projections, so that any potential reader will have the knowledge that not only are you proposing to grow the business, but you also have a plan. The financials will also include your exposure to licenses and fees for your professional registration.

Marketing Plan Structure

1. **Market Research**: Collate market information about products and services in your local area. Who is supplying products and services to your industry? What are competitors offering? What are the market demographics?

2. **Target Market**: Who is your target market? Who do you want to attract to your business?

3. **Products and Services**: Define the breadth of your offering. What are you selling or promoting to the market?

4. **Competitors**: What makes you stand out from the competitors? What makes you different and more desirable?

5. **Market Strategies**: How are you going to market your business e.g. networking, website, conferences, training programs, publishing articles, press releases and blogs, social media, advertising etc?

6. **Pricing and Branding**: Where will you be priced compared to your competitors? How will your branding stand you apart from others? Will your branding command a justified premium?

7. **Budget**: Yes, everything has a budget. What is your marketing budget and how will it be allocated? [9]

The Business Plan and Marketing Plan will become key foundations for your business. Firstly, if you are seeking finance for your business, a banking institution will want to see your business plans. Secondly, it becomes a reference point for you to return to at times when you feel that the business has gone off track. You have a plan. You have given due diligence to ensure that the plan is appropriate to where you want your business to be. Therefore, they will become the bedrock upon which you can grow.

Insurances and Regulations

This will depend on the modality of healthcare that you are offering, and also where you are geographically based. Every country and every state will have their own rules, regulations and licensing requirements. As mentioned above in the Business Plan (6), it will be incumbent upon you to ensure that you are registered and insured for the level of service that you offer.

---

9   https://www.businessknowhow.com/marketing/marketing-plan.htm

Would I benefit from having a business mentor or coach?

This is a question that is fraught with danger. At the time of writing this book, I had been working with a business mentor for over 12 months and it was one of the driving reasons for me to get out of procrastination mode to complete this book. She has also opened my mind to a new level of business elevation. So when considering the fact that my hypnotherapy practice was working to capacity and I didn't have any known scope for further growth, it was perfect timing for me to engage the services of someone to mentor me, to take me to new heights. I needed someone to shake me out of my comfort zone. So, the simple answer to the question above is YES.

> *"It's possible to love your business coach, but also be broke"*
>
> ~ Clay Clark (Thrive15.com)

If you are thinking of investing in a business coach, stop and ask yourself the following questions:

1. What do I want a coach to do, that I currently cannot do on my own?

2. Am I looking for a business coach or a therapist? "Rather than focusing on developing, marketing and selling products and services that people actually want to buy, many business coaching programs have essentially become quasi-psychologists for many lone-ranger entrepreneurs in search of somebody who will finally understand them and the inherent loneliness often associated with founding and growing a successful company."[10]

---

10   https://www.forbes.com/sites/forbescoachescouncil/2018/08/01/why-most-business-coaching-is-a-waste-of-time/#2d4f9cea631c

In the early days of my business, I engaged a business coach with the view of helping me to get established "in business". I was in transition phase from being employed to self-employed. There was a lot of mental adjusting to do and at the time, the business coach I chose was a perfect fit.

When deciding on a business coach, check out their testimonials and request a list of their clients or businesses. The coach you choose to work with has to be a good fit. There are many business coaches who are ready to sell you an off-the-shelf program, whereas you want someone who, in a short space of time, can help you to turn your business into a profitable and meaningful venture.

10 tips to Disaster-Proof Your Business

At the time of writing this book, the world was in the grip of the 2020 Coronavirus pandemic. Communities, economies, towns, cities, nations, people and businesses were being impacted upon in ways that no one living had ever experienced.

The initial waves of the pandemic hit the world so unexpectedly and swiftly, and with such magnitude, that many economies are still in the throes of a long, slow recovery. Small business suffered greatly, and indeed, some in our field are still working to stabilize and adapt their businesses as I write this. Unfortunately, some healthcare practitioners and their business will never recover.

So, is it possible to have strategies in place to plan for such an event?

For the purpose of this book, I will narrow the scope of that question to, *"How do we plan to protect our business in such an event?"*

Our business can be negatively affected by external forces at any time. Whether those forces are economic downturns, environmental impact from floods, fires or drought, or even an earthquake, it's incumbent on the individual business owner to have strategies in place to reduce any negative impact on their business in order to do what it takes to survive the threat.

In the event of such an occurrence, I encourage you to be flexible and creative, but also rational.

The following hands-on tips could be the steps you need to stabilize and minimize the impact on your business.

1. **Engage with your bookkeeper:** Speak with your accountant/bookkeeper to develop strategies for your business. Refer to your Business Plan. This might be the time to make changes to your business plan, to adjust your cash flow, to remodel your business, and in some parts of the world, apply for government assistance if it is available.

2. **Adjust your taxation commitment:** During the pandemic in Australia for example, you were able to temporarily suspend your Pay as You Go (PAYG) tax contributions for staff, or as a sole practitioner, paying yourself as an employee or taking drawings from the business. If this is the case for you, ask your accountant to apply to either have previous contributions returned from the Tax Office or discuss minimizing current and future payments. Other countries will have their own regulations, so please keep in contact with your accountant to discuss what is the best path for you to follow.

3. **Be disciplined with your diary:** Just because the number of face-to-face clients may reduce or disappear from your diary, it does not mean that you can have the day off. Apart from contacting your client base to let them

know that you're still open to help them and are now serving them online, this is the time to block off time in your diary for marketing and admin. Remember all those blogs and vlogs that you have always talked about writing or creating? In the words of Nike, the Greek Goddess of Victory … Just Do It! Create a daily "to do" list and tick off those business tasks. It might also be a time for you to freshen up your office space in readiness for new beginnings.

4. **Contact your Bank and Utility Suppliers:** Contact your bank to ask for a reduction in mortgage rates, a freeze on EFTPOS terminals, and a freeze on Merchant Fees. You will be pleasantly surprised at how amenable they can be. They want your business to survive. Contact utility companies (gas, electricity, water) to request reduction in bills in times of economic hardship. Shop around for the best deal for you.

5. **Contact your Rental Managing Agent** to request a three-month rental reduction. If you're renting your commercial premises or office, then in times of genuine financial stress, your managing agent is an early point of contact. They want you for the long term. If your business closes, they'll have an empty shop to lease out. Interestingly, at the time of writing this chapter, I had a call from a local healthcare practitioner who had negotiated a 50% reduction in her clinic rent.

6. **Contact and review software subscriptions** and ask for a moratorium on software rental payments. If you're like me, you will have subscriptions to several companies for software services to run your business. This is a time for rational thinking. It's a time to put on hold or close off subscriptions that your business doesn't need "right now". It doesn't mean that you have to cancel a subscription. It means that you can pause until the business cycle changes.

7. **Move your business online:** Be ready to move your business online by changing your approach from face-to-face to an online mode. This might take some adjustment,

however the business that can respond with flexibility in a crisis is the business that will survive the crisis. Make changes to your website and social media pages to reflect your new flexibility. Although I've been working with clients online (Skype/Zoom) for some years, it's usually been clients who live either remotely or live in another country. During the Coronavirus lockdown, all of my business moved to online services. This is the new business reality.

8. **Communicate with your market and client base:** Let them know that you're still there to provide assistance and will be there for face-to-face sessions when this crisis is over. Be clear and positive in your social media messages. This is a time for leaders to stand tall. This is an opportunity for you to be a leader in your market in the eyes of clients and the broader community. In times of crisis we can be the beacon of hope and positivity without being trite. When the community at large has had the foundations of their lives and livelihoods shaken, the one common need is consistent and instructive messaging. People want to know what to do.

9. **Network:** This is the perfect time to stay connected with other practitioners, to share and discuss creative ways of keeping your business afloat. Create or join online forums as there are many other healthcare practitioners who are seeking answers and solutions. This is a time for sharing ideas and systems. It's amazing how much I learned during the different stages of the pandemic and am still learning as the economy recovers. I now have the time to research and implement new systems that are strengthening my business. What I learn now is future proofing for anything that might follow.

10. **Breathe** … Be kind to yourself and others. Together, we will survive this, and we will return to a new kind of normal as countries around the globe recover, each at their own different pace.

Chapter 5 in Summary

This was the time to put on your business and marketing hats. It was the time to put solid plans in place that will become the foundation for your business to build upon.

Maximum Results: For those who are seeking maximum results from their business, I encourage you to take the time to create:

1. A Business Plan.

2. A Marketing Plan based on the structures as detailed in this chapter.

3. A crisis-proof business strategy to ensure you have developed online and off-line ways of treating your clients/patients and earning your income. No longer having a business that relies solely on the traditional face-to-face clinic model.

Print out your business and marketing plans. Put the plans in a folder that is dedicated to your business foundation. It will contain your blueprint for success, including business and marketing plans, templates for clients, and business registrations, insurances and licenses.

Note to self:

Don't file the business and marketing plan away, never to be seen again. This is important; it is the blueprint for your business success. You might find that there are times when your business or marketing direction is off course. By referring to your original plans, you might be surprised to find the answers were already there and it will become a great launchpad to keep moving forward.

Business and marketing platforms are forever changing and as such, every year you will have a need to have a fresh look at your business and marketing plans to gauge the current relevance of particular sections and to continue expanding into the future.

In the following Chapter, I introduce you to ways to systemize your business, whether to do budgeting, or software and communication styles. When you have systems in place, it will mean you save time and money on having to do things more than once.

TIP

Give free talks to community groups. It builds your network, and strengthens your industry status. Every time I speak to a community group, I end up with two or more new clients.

CHAPTER 6

Develop rock-solid strategies

> *"In reality strategy is actually very straightforward. You pick a general direction and you implement like hell."*
>
> ~ Jack Welch

We can all agree that the velocity of change is increasing at an exponential rate. Technological development is moving at light speed. The speed of changes in the way that we do business is caught up in that maelstrom, so to survive, we have to be fitter, smarter and more adaptive. If you don't adapt to change, then there is an increased chance that you will be left behind. As mentioned previously, business success is challenging, but you haven't come this far to fail. Have you?

> *"Hope is not a strategy."*
>
> ~ Vince Lombardi

Communication is King

Communication isn't just important; when it comes to your business, communication is everything. We are in the business of communicating with people every day. If you aren't communicating effectively, then that could be one of the prime reasons why your business is quieter than you would have liked. Communication is a multi-faceted beast and to be on top in business, you have to get all elements working in unison.

Digital communication

This is the first method of communicating to your potential client. They've done a search on Google, Yahoo or another search engine for your particular modality. (The finer details of your online communication were covered in Chapter 4, while digital advertising will be covered in Chapter 7.) Make sure your message is consistent and reflects you and your business. If you go off track and start delivering a message that doesn't reflect your business or the product or service that you're delivering, there is potential to lose your market's attention.

Verbal communication

Practice, Practice, Practice. A client has found you via a web search, a referral or maybe from one of your other marketing sources. They phone you to make an appointment or to gather more information. How do you answer the phone? I cringe when I call a business and the person answers saying, "Hello". I'm on my phone wondering, "Do I hang up now? Have I called the right number? Is this person really in business?" Thankfully this is a rarity, but you don't want that to be you. Take the view that you have one opportunity to win this client; or one opportunity to lose them.

I have a well-rehearsed script in my head, ready for the phone to ring. "Hi, this is Cameron Hypnotics, Brett speaking. How can I help you?" I have told them the name of the business, who they are speaking with, and I've invited them to join the conversation by asking how I can help them.

I encourage you to build up a short list of well-practiced patter, that you can roll off your tongue without sounding like a dodgy salesperson. It has to be authentic and said with meaning. This is not the time to sell anything to the client. This is the time to answer their questions, put their mind at ease knowing that they've found the right practitioner who can work with them, and lastly, ask them, "What day and time works best for you and I'll check my availability." Yes, at that stage I've put on my "sales hat" with the assumption that whenever someone phones me, it's a sale. If they don't make an appointment, then they were either just looking for information, or you have lost them.

Non-verbal communication

In 1970, American anthropologist Ray Birdwhistell published a book *Kinesics and Context*, based on his studies of inter-personal communication. Even though his studies were over five decades ago, his results are still widely referenced.

> 7% Words
> 38% Tonality
> 55% Body Language

His studies revealed that only 7% of effective communication is based on the words that we say; 38% is the way in which we say words and how we might emphasize certain words; 55% of effective communication is given to body language and facial expression. You might be thinking two words right now. So what? This is a time for you to reflect on your communication style and whether you are communicating to maximum effect. You can be hung up on finding the correct words when communicating, where maybe a more useful approach would be to just stop and observe what the other person is doing and how they're behaving and responding.

Rapport

Have you ever thought about what has happened when a conversation dies? What was missing that could have saved the moment? The answer is always rapport. I can still hear reverberating in my head the simple three-word phrase from my NLP teacher Laureli Blyth. She would repeat … "rapport, rapport, rapport." It's always my first focus when communicating with clients. I will quietly observe, acknowledge, and then communicate to reflect the manner in which they've communicated. It works every time. With one exception. You don't want to reflect anger back to a client who is expressing anger. Practice your rapport building skills. The more in tune you become, the better communicator you become.

Systems and strategies - How to work smarter, not harder

Accounting and Banking systems

First rule when starting a business is to get a good accountant. I've spoken with other healthcare practitioners who tell me that they have a bookkeeper and that they're more than happy with their services. However, I'm erring on the side of caution and suggesting you hire an accountant. It doesn't matter what country or state you are in, the accountant will:

- Have a working knowledge of government regulations and laws affecting your finances, e.g. tax structure, GST (Goods and Services Tax), VAT (Value Added Tax) and other consumption taxes.

- Be able to advise you on cash flow, inventory management and business financing.

- Be able to advise you on which on-line accounting software to choose. This might be MYOB, Quickbooks, Xero or others. I personally use Xero as I can administer it daily and when I make changes on any devices they all sync perfectly; and my accountant can access my account for tax purposes. Do your research and seek advice before committing. It has to be cost effective for you as well as having easy-to-use functionality. Ensure that your business bank account is linked to your accounting software.

Banking systems

Request a meeting with the business manager of your local bank or financial institution. This is a perfect opportunity to develop a business relationship with your banker. From my bank I required:

- A business bank account with low fees.
- A portable EFTPOS (Electronic Funds Transfer Point of Sale) machine.
- bankcard/credit card and cheque book.

You might be requiring a business loan, or maybe just seeking business advice. When I started in business, I was self-financed which meant that I was in a "sink or swim" scenario. When swimming with sharks you learn how to swim quite quickly. Always be on the lookout for cost saving options. Bank fees add up over time and if you can reduce that cost it will be to your benefit.

Budgeting

This is the dry area of the business that, if avoided, will be at your peril. Imagine that you are at the controls of a machine from the creative mind of Jules Verne. It's your business machine that is floating on an unknown sea littered with boulders, icebergs, and the skeletons of failed businesses. You have levers and pulleys to adjust, and dials and switches to correct; all to ensure that the business is not only afloat but is moving in a direction of your making. I have a running budget (Excel) that I tweak every day. It doesn't have to be complex. The objective is to have an idea at any one moment, of how my cash flow and monthly sales projections are situated. An example of a simple working budget based on projected monthly income and expenditure is:

BUDGET AS AT 10 JAN	INCOME (CREDIT)	EXPENDITURE (DEBIT)
Business Bank Acc.	$2,500	
Savings Acc.	$5,000	
Income To 22 Jan	$6,300	
Net Funds	$13,800 (Tally of above)	
Mortgage/Rent		$1500
Credit Card		$3000
Home Running Costs		$1300
Web Host		$50
Advertising		$500
Superannuation		$1500
Tax (Monthly)		$1000
Net Expenses		$8,850 (Tally of above)
Nett At 22 January	**$4,950**	

Therefore, from 10 January, from a simple reading of the spreadsheet I know that I can expect to have a nett balance of $4,950 by 22 January. It might mean that by the end of the month I will be able to allocate more money to savings, advertising or maybe let the cash flow build for the next two months.

By having a working budget I have flexibility in managing my business. If I found that potential income (forward projections) was looking lighter than I had hoped, I might be able to change my marketing plans, or trim my expenditure in an area that is not business related. It is all about adjusting the levers and pulleys.

Download a free Budget Template at:

www.youfullybooked.com/resources

Implementing strategies, systems and procedures

It doesn't matter from what field of the healing arts you belong; you could be a massage therapist, a chiropractor, a hypnotherapist, a counsellor, acupuncturist, or other. It is time to work smarter, not harder. There are many ways to not only semi-automate your business, but to lessen the often-repeated actions that take your precious time and energy. I've spoken with many successful therapists who trumpet the value of creating programs. Personally, I love the wisdom of offering individualized programs. For example, as a hypnotherapist, I offer a range of three to six session programs at a rate that's discounted from the session-by-session rate. It has many benefits to you and the client. Those programs are Anxiety Buster, Weight Release, Freedom from Gambling, Freedom from IBS, etc.

Benefits to the Client	Benefits to the Therapist
1. Perception that they have signed up for an already proven successful program.	1. You have a commitment from the client that they trust you to deliver the desired outcome.
2. They are saving money by committing to a program and paying up-front.	2. The money for three or more sessions is in the bank, therefore the client is committed to the program.
3. They have faith in a process of change.	3. You can mentally prepare for the client's sessions as you know what their goals are.

A successful chiropractor told me that he asks his patients to commit to an agreed program of six sessions. He then offers them bonuses or premiums at the end of the sixth session. He wants to establish a stronger list of longer-term patients. While he is competent at his craft, he wants to convert the short-term successes into long-term maintenance patients. This principle applies to any healing modality. Be creative and challenge yourself to offer multi-visit programs. You want to be seen as the expert in the field, not just another practitioner.

TIP

When stepping into a world of advertising spend, please read the sign at the entrance, "Enter at your own risk".

SEMI-AUTOMATED INTERNAL FORMS AND PROCEDURES:

How can you automate your business communications? Some areas that are high priority are:

1. Email responses: When a client emails you, have an automated response that says, "Hi, thank you for contacting me. I have received your email and I will respond more formally later today. Thank you for being patient."

2. Automated scheduling: Allow clients to book a session with you directly from your website, and also to pay you directly.

3. Automated appointment reminders: 48hrs prior to a client's scheduled appointment, have an automated SMS sent to the client's mobile/cell phone.

4. eForms: Allow your clients to complete intake or questionnaires on eForms that can be accessed online or offline. Be paperless.

The best resource would be to ask Google, YouTube, or Yahoo "how do I automate ...?" Speak with your web developer to gain insight into what software is compatible with your website. You might find, for example, that if you're using a Wordpress template, then there could be a pre-existing plug-in that solves the problem.

I have created a series of internal forms and questionnaires for my clients' use. I use Jotform as an online form builder, so clients can complete their intake electronically. A big time saver is the template system I've created for replying to clients' enquiries. As a hypnotherapist, I have tailored different word templates for smoking cessation, weight release, anxiety and also a generalized template. Therefore when a client has agreed to book an appointment, I email them a reply, insert the template into the reply, add the appointment days and times and hit "send". It's a good time saver and gives clear and concise information to the client including address, costs and information covering a cancellation fee. See an example below.

Thank you for contacting Cameron Hypnotics. I look forward to working with you as you move towards being free of symptoms of anxiety.

Confirming:

Session 1:	*(90 minutes)*
Session 2:	*(55 minutes)*
Session 3:	*(55 minutes)*

Cost:

If you choose to pay by session, the initial session is $xxx and the following sessions are $xxx each. I offer a 3 session program @ $xxx which is payable at the first session. I accept cash or card (Visa/Mastercard/Debit)

Where?

The practice is at xxx xxx Avenue, xxxxxx.

The following are links to iTunes and Spotify where I have a selection of Self-Hypnosis MP3s for download or stream. You would benefit from listening to the **Freedom from Anxiety – The Spinning Wheel** MP3.

https://itunes.apple.com/au/album/freedom-from-anxiety-spinning/id1037597152

https://open.spotify.com/album/3KtM0W8OAqYVqR0UFv8uLe

Alternatively, you can download the MP3 from my website. ($9.97)

https://cameronhypnotics.com.au/product/free-of-stress-and-anxiety-a-guided-self-hypnosis/

If you are unable to attend your appointment, please give me 24hrs notice so that I can allocate that time to another client. Failure to give adequate notice *might* attract a 50% session fee as I am allocating this time to you.

The following is a link to my Stop Smoking questionnaire on Jotform. https://form.jotform.com/Cameron_Brett/cameron-hypnotics---smoking-questio

Three simple systems that I have added are:

- Online form builder for clients to complete intakes and questionnaires.

- Online booking system. I use Timely. Clients can book a time online.
- Templates for replying to client enquiries.

Discipline: The missing ingredient

I work from a home office. I have my garden, which I love to disappear into. I have my library of books that I love to fold my mind and fingers around. I have my computer, which contains a myriad of canyons for me to explore. And don't get me started on Sudoku. I have a local shopping village a short walk away, where I can go and have a coffee or just allow my mind to wander. But I am also in business. My business coach asked me recently if I could clearly define one of the reasons why I have a successful hypnotherapy practice and business, while the majority of clinical hypnotherapists in Australia seem to be struggling. The answer that came to mind was discipline. While I believe that my passion and belief in being an effective hypnotist and therapist will help me to deliver a positive client experience, the key element that ensures that I am successful in business is to have a disciplined mindset.

I have found that the two key motivators for discipline are firstly, to have such a strong desire for success and a vision of you and your overflowing practice, that you are driven each and every day to succeed. Secondly, and this is relevant to people who have moved from being employed to now being the business owner, in the early stages of business I felt the need for accountability. For many years I was a part of a corporate management team and I had agreed responsibilities and accountabilities. When I left the security of being employed, it took some adjustment to transition into a position where I wasn't accountable to anyone.

In the introduction I told the story of the four business hats. They were the employee, the employer, the business owner, and you.

Each of those players is accountable to each other. The success of the business relies on all players in the team working together as a team and being accountable as a team. As mentioned, I had difficulties with accountability when I entered the business world. To remedy that problem I engaged with a business coach to whom I was accountable. In a short moment of time, I was able to create self-reporting processes which removed the problem.

How do I structure my day and working week? My overall weekly plan is based on seeing clients Monday to Thursday with a goal of seeing 20-24 clients each week. I have Friday as a client-free day, which I can then devote to marketing, administration, advertising, and of course, self-care.

My weekly schedule

Monday:	9:30am first client, 4:30 - 5:00pm last client (5-6 for the day)
Tuesday:	9:30am first client, 4:30 - 5:00pm last client (5-6 for the day)
Wednesday:	9:30am first client, 6:00pm last client (5-6 for the day)
Thursday:	9:30am first client, 6:00pm last client (5-6 for the day)
Friday:	Self-care, marketing, admin, PR, advertising.

My initial client session will run for up to 90 minutes, with following sessions being 50 minutes. Therefore, in a typical day, I can see five to six clients, have two half hour breaks and be finished by 6:00pm. I'm ready to start at 8:30am and will devote the next hour for client preparation, returning phone calls and email enquiries, as well as doing some last minute on-line marketing. In my mind, I'm devoting my day to the whole business. Interestingly, if I reflect back to a time when my practice wasn't so busy, I would suggest it was also a time when I didn't have the business discipline.

If I have a late cancellation, and I'm not able to fill that time slot, this is not wasted time. It means I have an hour to write a new blog, adjust a campaign, or ensure that my admin is up to date. There is always something that you can add to your business.

Resilience

I talk about personal resilience in Chapter 3, however it's important to have strategies in place to boost business resilience. Resilient people are less prone to being overwhelmed in a crisis. Therefore they are ready to act in a measured and controlled manner to optimize chances of recovery and success. This also applies to business. In a burgeoning healthcare practice, you also have to build in systems to ensure resilience. There might be times where, due to external economic forces that are out of your control, you experience a restricted business income. What do you do? Do you have a low cost marketing strategy in place? Do you have cash reserves to buffer the short-term pain? How diverse is your business offering? Maybe you can bolster one area while the other is rebuilding. Speak with other practitioners as you aren't the first healthcare practitioner to feel commercial strain.

Customer Relationship Manager (CRMs): Why are they important? Apart from having a filing cabinet full of client files and information, how do you know who your clients are? Every successful business has a CRM that is a key component of their everyday business and marketing activity. CRMs are centralized cloud based databases that allow you to:

1. Have a readily accessible record of your clients on any device.

2. Have a system where you can market directly to your entire client base or specific segments.

3. Invoice clients.

4. Have a system that has a unified Social Media manager built in. These systems can capture customer information from Facebook, Twitter, Instagram and other social media networks in a single interface so that you can communicate with your target audience.

Business success is based on maintaining relationships with your client. That success is predicated on how well we communicate with those clients.

My Story:

How easy is it to become overwhelmed with the pace of change? I've been to seminars, and I'm sure you have too, where a presenter is talking about changes to Facebook algorithms, and trending social media developments, as if "doesn't everyone know this?" A couple of months later, that same presenter will be talking about another technological leap. It can be daunting if you allow it to be.

In 2018, I had a 14-year-old boy as a hypnotherapy client who was experiencing anxiety because he had no idea what career he wanted. Okay, apart from juggling parental pressures, this lad was like a rabbit in the headlights of change. He was stuck.

I asked him if he had a smartphone. He showed me his latest Apple iPhone. I told him that the first iPhone was released when he was three years old. Facebook was launched the year that he was born. I suggested to him that perhaps, the career path he will choose hasn't been invented yet.

There are things that I was doing five years ago in business that are laughable now. My suggestion is that you don't have to embrace every new change that presents itself. However, if the opportunity arises, you have to put on your business hat and be prepared to adopt a system or strategy that will improve your business. Identify what can save you time and money, as well as help you to communicate more efficiently with your market.

Chapter 6 in Summary

This chapter has focused on building and applying systems of technology or communication that make your business more effective and streamlined. We have covered the application of:

- Better communication systems.
- Accounting and banking systems.
- CRMs.
- Automated systems.

The next chapter will flip the brain hemispheres again as you begin to explore the advertising and promotions minefield.

TIP

Practice gratitude every day. I start the day with a mini meditation expressing gratitude for my clients, my family, my health and the opportunities that my business gives me to grow.

CHAPTER 7

Step confidently into the online and print marketing and advertising minefield

> *"Making promises and keeping them is a great way to build a brand"*
>
> ~ Seth Godin

There is a caveat for this chapter. I am not responsible for how or what you advertise. I encourage the reader to be mindful of any restrictions or limitations that your particular profession places on you. As a hypnotherapist in Australia, I know that I can advertise and have more freedom with my content than some of my North American peers. However, chiropractors are restricted in what they can say in their advertising and on their website.

> *"Advertising without a way to sign up or book an appointment is like winking in the dark... It remains unseen"*
>
> ~ Dr Shelley Stockwell-Nicholas

Please do your research and check with your particular industry standards and regulations.

In August 2019, I had the pleasure of meeting successful therapist and coach, Dr. Shelley Stockwell-Nicholas at a conference in the United States. I asked her what tips she would give another therapist who was overwhelmed when confronted with the unlimited ocean of advertising options. Her key point was, "When marketing the good work you do, be an educator, not a blatant sales person." Moreover, she suggested:

1. **Sell Benefits:** People want to feel terrific. That's why they seek help. Let them know that people just like them report success with what you offer. Let them know that when they hire you, they will think more clearly and feel better in every way. Let them know that you are on their team to help them be their best. Your advertisements, announcements, website, blogs, literature and business cards have one thing in common: they need to answer the question "What's in it for me to hire YOU?"

2. **Get over yourself:** YOU are only their key and their tool for the results they want. You're an expert for THEM, it is not about you.

3. **Be personal:** Make your photo your logo. Put it on your business card. Otherwise your card becomes just another piece of junk. Look professional, friendly and accessible in your photo. Let your name personalize your work. Offer a signature protocol–your unique approach. Have your face and contact phone and email on everything you do. While that is Shelley's approach, and it's an approach that has worked for her, I personally don't like photos on business cards. The business card you choose to run with has to be a reflection of you and what you represent.

4. **Call to action:** Your clients need to be able to call, text, message or email you NOW, so everything you put out needs legible contact information. Put your contact information on every page of your website and on every page of your book or flyer. [11]

---

[11] Stockwell-Nicholas, Shelley, Excerpts from "Thrive", Creativity Unlimited Press, California, 2018.

Advertising and promotion is the area that seems to give new and not so new practitioners the biggest headache. When we look at the budget black hole, it is usually advertising and promotion that has swallowed all of your money. Remember the earlier message, if you don't have a skill in a particular area, find someone who does. Please be mindful that there is no proven formula for successful advertising. This is where you have to do your homework and research, as there are many digital marketers who are delivering a quality return, and likewise there are the cowboys who will take your money, promising the world, but instead delivering a second-hand atlas.

I was talking with a chiropractor recently who has now established himself with a healthy practice. He is professional and proficient at chiropractic and his solo business is steadily growing. Yet he is the first to admit that advertising and marketing his practice is not his strength. As such, he had entrusted a digital marketer to take responsibility for that arm of his business. He told me he was on his way to a meeting where he was going to end the relationship. Over the past six months he has contributed over $7,000 to digital marketing campaigns that have resulted in a possible five new clients. When I did a search on social media and Google for his business, it became increasingly depressing as I plowed through the pages trying to find his business.

Conversely, I know of a Queensland based hypnotherapist who is consistently contributing $750 per month to his Google adwords campaign which is administered by a third party. The third party is also managing the Search Engine Optimisation (SEO) on his website. This practitioner has nothing but praise and positive feedback for the marketing company and the advertising campaign. It works for him. He has a strong business relationship where they have open and flexible communications.

It wasn't always that way. Greg said that for a while he wasn't happy with the results from the provider. He complained numerous times and as a result his program was upgraded. The lesson in this is that you have to not only persevere, but also be ready to push the provider for an improved delivery of service.

The global focus for advertising is now on digital marketing. So, I ask the question, "Is print media dead?" Whenever I raise this question at workshops I get some polarized opinions. I know of healthcare practitioners who have run small block ads in their local newspaper and, for the small price that they're paying, feel it's been worthwhile. Others will tell me that this is something people did last century. Before you spend one cent on your advertising, do your research. Is your target market likely to read that newspaper? If you know that in your area, the demographic of newspaper readers is people aged over 55 who are semi or fully retired, and that is your target market, then of course that is the media of choice for you. If you are targeting a youth market, newspaper advertising to an older demographic is sending your advertising budget down the drain.

I have had a 15-month run of advertising success in a free local full-color life-style magazine that's distributed to cafes, community shopping centers, clubs and libraries. You have to match the media with your target market. This is also a great opportunity for your negotiation skills to come to the fore.

My advertising plan for print advertising

1. Find the media that fits my target demographic.

2. Research the businesses that have advertised in that magazine and ask some of them if it has been worthwhile. Businesses will generally be honest with other new businesses if there is no market conflict.

3. Get the rate card from the magazine and then negotiate a rate that you are happy with. I signed up for a three month (edition) contract where I paid for one-third of a page advertising. The magazine's graphic designer helped me with layout and design. Before I signed I also said I want to have a 600 word advertorial next to my advert. Voila! They agreed. I had a full page dedicated to my business.

4. I then got busy writing blogs/articles that would complement my advert, while also building a connection with the market as the expert in whatever the monthly topic was.

This was a magazine that has a monthly print run of 40,000. I knew that I needed just two clients a month from the advertising to pay for the outlay. It has been the most lucrative print media advertising venture that I have entered.

On-line vs. print? Or maybe co-existing?

If we measured by volume it could be said that social media advertising is in its ascendency and print advertising is stagnating. However, print is not dead. It holds a certain level of prestige.

- Wording and stories are limited so your promotional piece has to fit into a space.

- The digital world is transient. Therefore in a short period of time, your digital article can be moved until it is now out of sight, whereas, your print article is constant. It is there forever.

- In Australia, research has shown that 93% of shoppers who have thumbed their way through a physical catalogue will visit that store. [12]

---

12   O'Loughlin, Trish, "Social Media vs Print Advertising: Is Print Really Dead?" wmegroup.com.au/social

The digital marketer would argue that you can't track the performance of your print advertising compared to data tracking on digital advertising. For digital advertising you can track how many clicks, impressions, "likes" and actions that your ads have generated. This allows you the freedom to edit your campaign to fit with what is working and what is not.

Social media writer Trish O'Loughlin, suggests that the two forms of media, if used effectively, can work to complement each other. She suggests that you can:

1. Use print media to direct audiences to your online platforms. Take advantage of your print appearance to showcase your online presence. Always list your social media URLs, hashtags etc.

2. Use social media to promote your print success. Amplify your success by adding social tags. Tell the digital world about your print success. [13]

Facebook Advertising

Whether you like or dislike Facebook, it's so dominant in social media that you cannot ignore it. Let's dissect some **Facebook statistics**. [14]

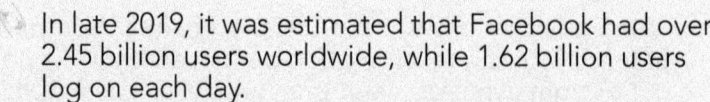

- In late 2019, it was estimated that Facebook had over 2.45 billion users worldwide, while 1.62 billion users log on each day.

- In Europe, over 307 million people are on Facebook.

- Australia has over 17.1 million people using Facebook.

13   Ibid, O'Loughlin, Trish.
14   https://zephoria.com/top-15-valuable-facebook-statistics/

- 25-34 is the most common age demographic, representing 29.7% of users.
- Highest Facebook traffic is between 1:00-3:00pm mid-week.
- Thursdays and Fridays engagement is 18% higher than other days in the week.
- Average time spent on Facebook is 20 minutes.
- 42% of marketers said Facebook is critical to their business.
- One out of five page views in the United States is on Facebook.
- Facebook owns WhatsApp, Instagram and Messenger.

So, the question I ask is, if you don't have a Facebook Business page and you aren't using it every day, how many potential clients and customers have just passed you by? I was at a hypnotherapy workshop in early 2019, and we had a moment to discuss how to attract clients. I was amazed when a few people raised their hands saying that they didn't have a Facebook page, while one person said she didn't even have a website. Hmmm. Maybe, that was one of the reasons why I felt the need to write this book.

You're advertising on Facebook to make a profit and you do that by capturing an audience and then having a call to action.

> *"Your ad copy is there to sell the click-through, not the product or service. So don't go on a long-winded explanation of features, benefits and outcomes. Instead, (a) grab attention and (b) create enough intrigue so people click through for more. That's it. Nothing less, and nothing more."*
>
> ~ Brad Smith (AdEspresso) [15]

Smith further states that for best results, your ad post text should have 14 words, while your link description has 18 words. Keep it simple and straightforward.

How much money do you throw down the Facebook rabbit hole? Hey, I've been there. I've created a beautiful ad on Facebook, I had a targeted campaign and I had an untold number of likes. At the end of the campaign spend, Facebook dutifully asked, "Do you want your ego to be stroked again for another $100?" And what did I do? Of course, I lay down while Facebook scratched my belly, whispered sweet nothings and took my money. I've learned a lot from that experience. Before we look at how to structure your online ad campaign, let's get the hazards out of the way: [16]

- You don't have any goals.
- You're using the wrong ad format.
- You only have one ad set.
- Your targeting is too broad.
- You don't get to the point.
- You use too much text in your ad.
- Your images aren't optimized for Facebook.
- Your images aren't eye catching.
- You aren't testing your ads.
- You're saturating your audience.

---

15   Smith, Brad in https://www.forbes.com/sites/sujanpatel/2017/02/04/10-mistakes-newbies-make-with-paid-facebook-ads/#37d6dcd92d2a

16   Patel, Sujan in https://www.forbes.com/sites/sujanpatel/2017/02/04/10-mistakes-newbies-make-with-paid-facebook-ads/#37d6dcd92d2a

The simple rule for anyone entering into the arena of Facebook advertising, is to either dive in and learn as much as you can before you start spending money, or find someone who knows what they're talking about. Please ensure the person you choose will not cost you the earth.

Steps to a low cost Facebook campaign:

- What is the goal of the campaign?
- What is your budget? How far are you prepared to go?
- Create your graphic that fits Facebook advertising guidelines.
- Create a video. Facebook loves videos.
- Create your copy to fit Facebook advertising guidelines.
- What is your target demographic? Who do you want to see your ad?
- Do you have a call to action?
- Ask people to comment and share. Then reply to their comments.

"Live" videos: If your goal is purely to boost your organic reach and to broaden your market base, then without spending money on Facebook advertising, you might consider generating "live" videos. Live videos get up to six times more interaction as regular video content. Practice in front of your camera. Make sure that lighting is good, and your voice is clear (with no background noise as a distraction), and begin your video.

Tips for Facebook "lives"

1. Introduce yourself. Where are you from? Why you?

2. Introduce your message. What is your purpose?

3. Share the message. Give the viewer something to take away.

4. Ask people to like and share.

5. Tell people who you are again. Engage with the audience and don't forget to thank them. Post it.

6. Then go into Facebook and do your editing. Give your video a title and description. Add a comment from yourself and ask viewers to comment on something that you feel is relevant to your video and message.

Doing "live" videos is not just any video. It is one component of your overall marketing strategy. You might create a theme where for the next month your core focus for marketing will be on one area of your business, e.g. a massage therapist might have a "March Massage for Mums Month". Therefore weekly "live" videos will be created on the theme of attracting mums to your practice. Remember the call to action. If you don't have a call to action, then what was the point of the video?

Other media

Where should I advertise and what should be avoided? Invariably when speaking to other practitioners, I will be asked that question. The simple answer is "whatever works for you." There are so many avenues to pursue and each of them could be a costly exercise. Enter with caution.

Letterbox drop: You have gone to a lot of effort and cost to design and print a flyer that advertises your business. You then decide that these flyers should go into everyone's letterbox because everyone wants to know about my business. That is NOT targeted marketing. That is HOPE marketing. If you speak with any Real Estate agent who uses the letterbox drop system, they will tell you that the uptake is approximately 1%. If you think that a 1% conversion of your marketing spend is acceptable then go for it. I would suggest that this is lazy and wasteful marketing.

Shop-a-dockets: What is your target demographic? To advertise my services on the back of a supermarket docket is not the market that I am attracting. I have not met a healthcare practitioner who has advertised successfully in this medium.

Pharmacy Prescription covers: Oh, the mistakes I have made. Many years ago I was called at a weak and vulnerable moment. I purchased one side of a Pharmacy Prescription cover from a prominent pharmacy near me, for a six-month period. The idea was that I would have my name on 4500 prescription covers. I didn't get one enquiry. Not one. Lesson learned.

Charity magazines: I support charities whenever I can. Active philanthropy is a beautiful way of giving back to society and the community with the goal to helps others to grow. I suggest that you consider advertising in charity-focused media, only if it serves you and your business. This is a moment for engaging the three brains. If you don't get three green ticks of approval, then don't do it.

Free websites: As a start-up business it sometimes makes sense to throw your marketing net wide as you might have limited marketing dollars to spend. Every country has lists of websites that will give you a free listing, e.g. Yellow.com. However, be mindful that Google and other search engines might punish you if you over expose yourself. You could find that your business name and URL is soon sliding down the search engine pages.

Chapter 7 in Summary

Advertising is promoting you and your service. It's a call to clients to trust in you to deliver them from their problem. But how much should you spend on advertising and marketing? The U.S. Small Business Administration recommends that a small business should spend between 7-8% of your gross revenue on marketing and sales. For someone starting up, you could calculate that as a percentage on your projected gross revenue. Your marketing and advertising spend includes:

- Brand.
- Website design and development.
- Marketing strategy.
- Advertising.

It could be argued that if you aren't prepared to invest at least 5% of your income in advertising and marketing, then perhaps you aren't really in business.

TIP

Review your advertising ... even if it's working. It's your investment so you have to be ready to steer your ship on a different course when your instincts tell you. Once advertisers have you in their grip, they won't let go easily.

Maximum Results Activity: For maximum results, I encourage you to create an Advertising/Marketing budget. For this exercise, let's suggest that you have an income projection of $100,000 p.a.

Website development + Maintenance. (one-off)	$4,000
Mail Manager	$240
Marketing subscriptions	$360
Google Adwords	$3400
CRM Subscription	$500
Facebook Marketing	$1,000
Business Cards and Flyers	$750
Magazine/Newspaper advertising	$1,250
Signage/Branding	$500
Total 8% of Income (exc. website – one off)	$8,000

Wow! When I look at that budget I can see areas that don't make sense. I suggest that in the first year, the bulk of your expenditure will be skewed towards the one-off costs such as website development and printing of signage. Everything else is ongoing costs.

It doesn't leave much for your digital marketing investment, so you have to either be frugal, or be prepared to spend more on advertising and marketing in your startup year. Do the exercise yourself. Remember the budget exercise in Chapter 6. It's important to keep your budget at front of mind. This is you wearing the various business hats.

What happens if you fall over? Who is going to pick you up? The next chapter brings the focus to you and self-care. The most important single person in your business is you. Let's focus on you and your wellbeing, to ensure that you will be there to celebrate the hard yards that you have worked so diligently to achieve.

TIP

Create a picture in your mind of how you would like to see you and your business in three years. Be that person now.

CHAPTER 8

Self-care: who is looking after you?

> *"Self-care is how you take your power back."*
>
> ~ Lalah Delia

I was thinking recently about the words of my mentor Maggie Wilde, when she said, "The moment you cheer when a client cancels an appointment, is the moment you know that you are overstretched." As a healthcare practitioner, that can sometimes be a good problem to have. A catalyst for me wanting to write this book was an "aha" realization I had after stopping to reflect on my own personal and business goals.

When I moved back to my home city of Newcastle, Australia in 2012, my vision, dream and goal was to have a fully booked and successful hypnotherapy practice where I was earning my goal income, and to have a balanced and happy life. At that time of reflection I realized I had achieved all. While it's great to have a moment to pop the champagne cork and to celebrate successes and achievements, it was also a time to apply energies to the next stage of my personal and business development.

I have to attribute a part of my success story to the fact that I put self-care in my diary every week. I'll be the first to admit that it wasn't always that way. It's natural to want to apply every possible hour to your business in order to maximize income and to grow your business. Everyone wants to be successful. There's nothing wrong with that. But it does become problematic when you notice that:

1. Your health is suffering.

2. Your job performance is slipping and you start to question whether you have been 100% present with your client/patient.

3. Your family and personal life balance is out of kilter.

4. Elements of your overall business plan are withering from neglect.

As mentioned in Chapter 6, I apply a systemized approach and have developed my own organizational structure for planning my day. After 14 years in business, I am still flying solo. I do the marketing, the advertising and the admin. I greet the clients, and I'm the only practitioner in my business, so I'm the one who sees the clients. At the time of writing, I was seeing on average between 20-24 clients per week. So, let's look at **strategies for self-care**.

1. **Diarize time off**. When I knew I was facing burnout, I decided to cut my face-to-face client days down to four days a week. I have Fridays as a client-free day. It's a day where I'll make time for a walk to the beach, a swim, a massage, a visit once a month to my chiropractor, a coffee with a friend, or maybe just make time to sit down with a book. However, it's also a day when I will do two to three hours of admin and marketing work. My Friday is the day for me to allocate time to work *on* the business, not *in* the business.

2. **Never ever see clients on your weekend**. Remember this is my rule. You might decide that your weekend is Sunday-

Monday. It doesn't matter what days you set aside, it's all about you prioritizing you and making sure that when a client contacts you saying, "I know that this is your day off, but this is important", that you stop, take a deep breath and give that client your next available time slot. I have also been challenged by that situation many times. Remember to schedule "joy" into your diary. It might be family or spouse time, or it might be time to spend on something that makes you happy.

3. **Make time for spiritual balance.** Whether it be meditation, yoga, prayer, mindfulness or just time for contemplation, you need to clear your head to allow yourself to just be. I know of a practitioner who likes to swim laps of the pool to clear their head.

4. **Practice gratitude.** Sometimes we can be so focused on what can go wrong, or be focused on the stresses of the day, that we can lose sight of the beautiful things in our lives. Every morning before my first client I take the time to tap (EFT) on the karate chop area of my left hand while repeating a gratitude mantra. It might be something like, "I am grateful for my loving family, I am grateful for the abundance of fresh food and water that I have, I am grateful for the air that I breathe, I am grateful for the clients that my business is attracting etc." It gets my mind and body into a ready and focused state for the day.

5. I like to have a day off during the week so that I can have the weekend to focus on being with **family and friends**. I know that although I have given myself the day away from clients, there have been many Fridays where I've spent many hours at my desk creating marketing campaigns, catching up on admin work as I enter my week's client details into my CRM, tweaking my website, or writing blogs and articles.

6. **Self-care** can include making time to engage in a sport or outdoor activity that you love. You might go out bushwalking or hiking, have a round of golf, go to the movies, give some time to your garden or your favorite

craft, or get creative in the kitchen. Loosen the strings, take your mind out for a walk and engage the parts of your mind and body that haven't been utilized this past week. Take your brain out for a creative experience. I find that my creative energy is sparked by walking through an art gallery or a nature reserve. As a storyteller, I crave finding a metaphor in something that others might find inane and nondescript.

Chapter 8 in Summary

The allocation of dedicated time to self-care is very important. Think of the airplane analogy. There is a beautiful logic to the words of the stewards when they say, "When the oxygen mask comes down, put yours on first". Of course, you can't save anyone if you have passed out. This also applies to your business, particularly if you are the only one in the business. Your on-going health maintenance is one thing that people forget to include in their Business Plan.

- Diarize time for you.
- Diarize your annual holiday.
- Create savings for 13 months, not 12 months.
- Seek life balance.
- Have a Fully Booked practice.

TIP

Greet your client/patient and ask them the golden question, "Are you ready for some positive hypnosis today?" "Are you ready for a positive adjustment today?" "Are you ready for a great massage today?" Create a positive greeting in words that feel comfortable to you. You have already sown the seeds of change in the client's mind.

PRACTITIONER BLOOPERS

Did they really say or do that?

I have loved writing this book. It's been a journey of fun, stress, writer's block, clarity, moments of flow where the words just flowed onto the page, and sometimes all of that in one session.

One of the mantras that has got me through is, "Lighten up!"

To gain a greater insight, I've interviewed and spoken with many practitioners as I collated the content and ideas for this book. One of the common threads that we all have as healthcare practitioners is that we have all made mistakes. It's just one of those things that makes us human.

The following real stories have been provided by an amazing group of practitioner colleagues from around the world. I've pulled together a compilation of some of the moments when each of us, from many fields, had "one of those" moments.

I'm sure you know the moments I'm talking about, moments when they cringed about something they said or didn't say while working with a client, did or didn't do in a session, and even the many things that were simply out of the practitioner's control.

As we laughed and reminisced over the tales of these real stories, there was one thing each of these practitioners agreed we had in common, *we could all look back and laugh – NOW!"*

Thanks for inviting me into your world and trusting me to be on your journey with you.

Bloopers and Outtakes:

1. **Shelley Stockwell-Nicholas**

   I did a stellar session with a very nice lady. I was erudite, and concise and I knew I had nailed it. I had reprogrammed her inner mind perfectly for one solid hour. When she was back in room awareness, she said, "I am sorry Dr Shelley but I am hard of hearing and I didn't hear a word you said." Lesson learned… Now I insist that I and my students SPEAK UP!

2. **Chiropractor (name withheld)**

   Many years ago, and I still laugh at this, I was working with a client. They were lying on the adjustment bed, I asked them to roll over, and in doing so, their left arm bent at an unnatural angle. I was momentarily horrified and then broke into uncontrolled giggles when I realized it was their prosthetic arm.

3. **Acupuncturist**

   I won't name the acupuncturist, as I was the patient. Many years ago I had a session of acupuncture and had walked to the reception area to pay. It was at this point that the receptionist called the acupuncturist to the reception, as she'd noticed a pin sticking in my forehead, like an antenna. Oops.

4. **Brett Cameron (yes, that's me)**

   As a hypnotherapist I was seeing a client for anxiety. The client had drifted into a wonderful state of hypnosis, and I think I had too. I must have brought myself out of hypnosis when I heard the words echoing in my head, "And you'll never smoke again". Later when the client opened her eyes, she smiled knowing that she would never smoke again … even though she had never smoked in her life.

5. **Maggie Wilde – The Potentialist**

   This was my first ever paying client after placing a two-line ad in a newspaper. Stop smoking with hypnosis and the phone number. I had an enquiry from a smoker who needed a home visit. A husband and wife both wanted a session at the one time. I was overtly anxious but said yes. I forgot to organize the environment, e.g. telephone turned off, kids, dog – it was a disaster … phone rang, kids were home, dog started licking client's hand. I couldn't get out of there fast enough. I ran home embarrassed and swore off treating smoking clients ever again, and stopped the ad in the local paper. About three months later I had a call from a man wanting to book in for smoking. It was the couple's friend – they'd never smoked again. Moral is, never be afraid to follow up.

6. **Freddy Jacquin**

In my early days as a hypnotherapist, the majority of my clients were in my office to quit smoking. At one point I was seeing between six to eight smokers a day and was booked six weeks in advance. My quit smoking protocol, apart from personalization, follows pretty much the same pattern for each smoker.

One day after having seen four or five smokers in a row, I was going through my usual routine and words. What I meant to say, to the client, who was deep in hypnosis at this point and taking on-board all of my suggestions, was, "When you leave here today the thought of a cigarette will be gone from your mind and you will be free of the habit forever".

What I actually said though was, "When you leave here today, the need for a cigarette will be gone, and you will be out of your MIND forever".

Still, I'm only human, and you can never have too many crazies in the world, otherwise it would be boring.

Oh, I love looking back… hindsight is a marvelous thing indeed. I thank each of the practitioners above for allowing me to share their stories.

7. Jason Linett

Sometimes the change in a hypnosis session goes beyond why they initially called you.

A friend in the profession named Melissa Tiers starts her process by asking the client "What do you want to change today?" Those familiar with hypnotic language patterns will notice the embedded command of "change today" at the end of the sentence.

I used this question with a client, and the emotions flowed as we talked about letting go of stress around a difficult situation with her sister. She processed phenomenal themes of forgiveness and reclaimed her confidence in the hypnosis session.

At the end of the appointment, she said, "that was amazing!" This woman genuinely looked twenty years younger as her face wasn't carrying the burden of this stress anymore. She continued, "but what about the weight loss stuff?"

Oops.

I had become swept into the narrative of this challenging conflict with her sister. I never once thought to look at her office forms. She was coming to me for hypnosis for weight loss! She had hired me to help her curb nighttime snacking and increase her motivation to exercise.

"But what about the weight loss stuff?"

Inspiration kicked in as I responded, "Yes, I've found greater success by first clearing away the emotional triggers and then addressing the specific habits and behaviors."

"Wow, that's brilliant!" she replied. Oh good, she bought it. Remember, it's only a mistake if you say the word "oops."

She was easily losing weight as our hypnotic processed continued. Still, whenever I'd ask for feedback as to how well things were going between appointments, she's only briefly touch on the weight loss success. She talked more of the changes in her life as she reconciled with her sister.

The kicker to the story? A few months passed and the phone rang one morning with a new client inquiry coming in by way of referral.

"I'd like to know if you can help me quit smoking? My sister says you changed her life."

Wow. This stuff works.

How to Have a Fully Booked Practice – a Bonus

Here's a selection of bonus tips to ensure your business is Fully Booked.

- Cash reserves: Start a new business with at least six months cash reserves. If you plan to be working part-time as you have another job, you might only need three months cash reserve.

- When handing a business card to a client, always give them two. Ask them to hand one card to someone who they know would benefit from your services.

- Always get appointment confirmations from your clients. They will know that you are prepared for them, and secondly nobody wants a "no show".

- Give free talks to community groups. It builds your network, and strengthens your industry status. Every time I speak to a community group, I end up with two or more new clients.

- Practice gratitude every day. I start the day with a mini meditation expressing gratitude for my clients, my family, my health and the opportunities that my business gives me to grow.

- Create a picture in your mind of how you would like to see you and your business in three years. Be that person now.

Greet your client/patient and ask them the golden question, "Are you ready for some positive hypnosis today?" "Are you ready for a positive adjustment today?" "Are you ready for a great massage today?" Create a positive greeting in words that feel comfortable to you. You have already sown the seeds of change in the client's mind.

Review your advertising … even if it's working. It's your investment so you have to be ready to steer your ship on a different course when your instincts tell you. Once advertisers have you in their grip, they won't let go easily.

When stepping into a world of advertising spend, please read the sign at the entrance, "Enter at your own risk".

When choosing a CRM, do your homework. They can range from close to free to $100 per month or more. What do you need now, and is there flexibility for future growth?

References

Bibliography:

Bandler, Richard, *Using Your Brain for a Change*, Real People Press, Utah, 1985

Stockwell-Nicholas, Shelley, Excerpts from "Thrive", Creativity Unlimited Press, California, 2018

Whitmore, John, *Coaching for Performance*, Nicholas Brealey Publishing, London, 2004

Web References:

Griffiths, Erin, "Why start ups fail, according to their founders", Fortune.com, September 25, 2014

O'Loughlin, Trish, "Social Media vs Print Advertising: Is Print Really Dead?" wmegroup.com.au/social

Patel, Sujan in https://www.forbes.com/sites/sujanpatel/2017/02/04/10-mistakes-newbies-make-with-paid-facebook-ads/#37d6dcd92d2a

Smith, Brad in https://www.forbes.com/sites/sujanpatel/2017/02/04/10-mistakes-newbies-make-with-paid-facebook-ads/#37d6dcd92d2a

https://www.businessknowhow.com/marketing/marketing-plan.htm

https://www.entrepreneur.com/article/38290

https://www.forbes.com/sites/forbescoachescouncil/2018/08/01/why-most-business-coaching-is-a-waste-of-time/#2d4f9cea631c

https://blog.hubspot.com/blog/tabid/6307/bid/23454/the-ultimate-cheat-sheet-for-mastering-linkedin.aspx

https://sociallysorted.com.au/7-reasons-why-i-love-instagram/

https://zephoria.com/top-15-valuable-facebook-statistics/

Acknowledgments

There are so many people whose presence and influence over the decades has left a positive and lasting impact on me, both professionally and as a private citizen. First and foremost, I want to acknowledge the faith and trust of my thousands of clients and patients from the past decade and a half. They are my daily teachers.

As a hypnotherapist, I couldn't have started this journey without the wisdom and truth of my hypnotherapy teacher and mentor, the late David Kennedy. He was a beautiful man and an inspirational soul. When I approached him to attend his Brisbane school, the words from that initial interview still ring true today. He said, "I don't want average students. If you don't have the passion and drive to be the best, then don't bother." Thank you.

Since those early days I have been blessed to have observed and studied with some of the contemporary leaders of the hypnosis world. I have honed the skills of my craft as well as enhancing my business and marketing abilities. Some of those I give thanks to are Stephen Brooks, Freddy Jacquin, Bob Burns, Mike Mandel, Jason Linett, Rob McNeilly, Roy Hunter, Laureli Blyth, and Karl Smith. Thank you to the book's contributors who kindly gave their time, words and wisdom that adds depth to this book. I acknowledge my first business manager, Stuey Alderman, who gave me my first start in business way back in 1987. He was a great people teacher. He taught me how to read people, how to communicate and how to facilitate with confidence.

I give thanks to my publisher Maggie Wilde-The Potentialist and her team at Mind Potential Publishing. Thank you for trusting in this project. Maggie has given me both the freedom and guidance for me to produce this book. I thank my dearly departed first wife Cynthia for her inspiration for me to pursue the field of hypnotherapy. And I give thanks to my darling wife, Afaf Girgis AM for her love, support and encouragement. She also provided the coffee and meals as well as the "are you procrastinating?" reminders from time to time.

I am thankful to the many who I have not named. You know who you are.

Meet the Contributors

Jason Linett

Be everywhere. Duplicate yourself. Make it rain.

Jason Linett has created a model of what it means to "Work Smart." At any point in time, people might be reading his words, watching his videos, or listening to his audios. This continues even while he's personally working with a client in his hypnosis business or he's at home with his family… or even asleep!

He is a best-selling author of WORK SMART BUSINESS: Lessons Learned from HYPNOTIZING 250,000 People and Building a MILLION-DOLLAR Brand. The book instantly dominated a #1 spot in several business categories on Amazon.

He is a TEDx speaker, a full-time professional hypnotist, and the host of the WORK SMART HYPNOSIS PODCAST, a program with more than a million downloads worldwide in more than 80 countries.

Jason has received major awards as the "Hypnotist of the Year' by the Mid-America Hypnosis Conference and "Faculty Member of the Year" by the National Guild of Hypnotists.

He is an internationally sought-after speaker as he has presented talks and inspirational keynotes at dozens of conferences worldwide.

Jason Linett is an educational pioneer in the world of hypnotherapy. His online educational programs, HYPNOTIC WORKERS and HYPNOTIC BUSINESS SYSTEMS are used by thousands of professional hypnotists worldwide.

While building a successful business is a great goal to strive toward, Jason is most proud of his ability to do so and be at home each night with his wife and two children.

For a free collection of resources connected to this book, visit WorkSmartHypnosis.com/Brett

Laureli Blyth is a certified, accredited international Master Trainer and Master Practitioner of NLP. The founder and director of the Australasian Institute of NLP in Sydney Australia, Laureli has been involved with NLP since 1983. She has studied and worked with a number of respected leaders in NLP and has trained thousands of people around the World. She has written several books, including *Numerology of Names, Brain Power, Dream Power, 30 Days to NLP, Neuro Intelligence* and co- authored *You Must Learn NLP*. She has always been fascinated with the mind and brain and how different forms of energies affect human beings.

www.nlpworldwide.com

Jason Gemenis is the creative lead at Peppermint Digital - a design business he co-founded in 2000. For the last 20 years, he has worked with agencies and brands on how to create and maintain a user-focused experience for their products and services. During that time, he has also taught with the next generation of digital designers as a lecturer at Sydney's Macleay College.

www.linkedin.com/in/jasongemenis/

Dr. Shelley Stockwell-Nicholas is President of the International Hypnosis Federation and has been a full time hypnotherapist for 40 years. She is the author of 24 books on how to be happy, healthy and successful (four of these co-authored with her friend the venerable Ormond McGill). Shelley speaks at universities and is a regular guest on radio and television talk shows.

www.hypnosisfederation.com

Melanie Morschel has a strong background in WordPress, SEO training and has built, owned and managed two award winning small tourism accommodation businesses. Melanie believes it is important for business owners to have the ability to easily manage their websites (if they want to!). Not only does she deliver beautiful, functional websites, she also equips clients with the tools they need to own their online space. She's been using WordPress to create small business websites for over 10 years, and believes it's the best Content Management System (CMS) on the market.

www.rapidwebsites.com.au

Freddy H Jacquin, founded the UK Hypnotherapy Training College in 1999, now known as the Jacquin Hypnosis Academy. He has personally worked with and helped more than 30,000 clients. Freddy has trained hundreds of students on five continents to become effective hypnotherapists. His book, *Hypnotherapy* has sold thousands of copies, worldwide. He is probably best known for "The Arrow Technique", which enables people to eliminate chronic physical and emotional pain.
Freddy is also the father of one of the world's foremost hypnotists/hypnotherapist, Anthony Jacquin, with whom he runs the Jacquin Hypnosis Academy.

https://freddyjacquin.com

Meet the Author

In 2006, Brett left a corporate career in sales and marketing, to pursue a dream. He studied and trained in Hypnotherapy and NLP, and he knew that he couldn't be held back. Brett has a thriving Clinical Hypnotherapy practice in Newcastle, Australia. He is back in his hometown after spending many years in Sydney. He loves a work-life balance. If he isn't seeing clients, or working on the marketing/admin side of the business, he could be seen early mornings walking his miniature schnauzer along the local beaches with his wife. Maybe you'll find him with a coffee in one hand while reading a book in the garden. He has a quest for knowledge and is always pushing himself to grow. Brett is a professional practitioner, a mentor, public speaker and an author.

www.cameronhypnotics.com

www.youfullybooked.com

www.hypnoticsacademy.com

TIP

You'll find helpful FULLY BOOKED Free Resources from Brett Cameron at:

www.youfullybooked.com/resources

What People Say...

"Brett is an outstanding hypnotherapist and coach. His warm and encouraging nature really brings out the best in people. Brett has trained with the world's best and brings a phenomenal level of expertise to his work. If you are looking to make positive life changes I highly recommend you get Brett on your team."

~ **Rebecca Moore** (Clinical Hypnotherapist Trance Works NZ)

"I met Brett a few years ago while attending an Ericksonian hypnotherapy course in Thailand. We had an instant connection and have since worked together to deliver an inspirational hypnosis workshop in Cardiff. Brett is a warm person and a master at his craft. If you're in Australia, or anywhere for that matter, and want to be the best version of you then seek out Brett Cameron to help you, highly recommended."

~ **Stephen Truelove** (Love Life Love You, Cardiff Wales)

"Thanks, Brett, for your invaluable help mate. I feel like a new man. I can't thank you enough and also my kids have bounced back into my life with my new outlook. Thank you."

~ **Jason Smith** (Jewells)

"I cannot recommend Brett enough for giving me the resources I needed to help me recognize and effectively deal with stressful situations, both in my professional life and my personal life as well."

~ **Graeme Taylor** (Asia Pacific Corporate Manager)